Praise for *Thrifty Green*

"This inspirational guide demonstrates the extent to which thrifty living and green living truly go hand in hand. The advice and stories here give us all the tools to bring 'off-grid' thinking and practices to our 'on-grid' lives. And save money, and precious natural resources, in the process."

—Califia Suntree and Pia Catton, coauthors of
Be Thrifty: How to Live Better with Less

"If you want to stay in denial and apathy, if you want to rationalize self-destructive patterns, this book's not for you. On the other hand, if you want to know how to reduce your spending and your carbon footprint while increasing the joy and the beauty in your life, if you want to live a low-cost, high-happiness life, you could not ask for a finer guide than this marvelous book."

—John Robbins, author of *The Food Revolution,*
Diet for a New America, and *The New Good Life*

"*Thrifty Green* reads like a letter from an old friend sharing fascinating news about her experiment in tiny-footprint living. It is inviting rather than inveighing, refreshing rather than depressing. She provides more information than most 'how-to' or 'why-to' books on frugality, yet it feels more like going on an adventure with her, trying on her choices to see if they fit."

—Vicki Robin, author of *Your Money or Your Life*

"Both a compelling narrative and a collection of sage advice, *Thrifty Green* represents the next step in sustainable thinking—and it couldn't come at a better time."

—Vanessa Farquharson, author of *Sleeping Naked Is Green*

"The motivating voice of *Thrifty Green* is a new generation making it cool to care about conservation. With an integrated perspective of the systems, large and small, that govern our framework on energy use, water, trash, transportation and consumable goods, this book infuses a willing attitude for smart, sound, more sustainable ways of living. Without forfeiting comfort or convenience, *Thrifty Green* offers strategic, painless ways to conserve, conscious decision making, and helpful factoids that make the journey much more than the sum of its parts."

—Renée Loux, author of *Easy Green Living*,
co-founder of Andalou Naturals

"You don't have to be rich or a rock star to figure out that living lighter is a lot more fun, healthier, and less expensive than you expected. *Thrifty Green* lays out the road. And you don't even need a bike or an electric car to drive there (though I'd recommend it)."

—Chris Paine, director of *Revenge of the Electric Car* and *Who Killed the Electric Car?*

"Far more than just a practical primer for those with an interest in living lighter on the planet, *Thrifty Green* succeeds in capturing a true sense of place and presents a compelling case for why living more simply can be the richest lifestyle choice of all."

—Jeff Yeager, author of *The Cheapskate Next Door* and
The Ultimate Cheapskate's Road Map to True Riches

Thrifty Green

Ease Up on Energy, Food, Water,
Trash, Transit, Stuff—and
Everybody Wins

Priscilla Short

Conari Press

First published in 2011 by Conari Press,
an imprint of Red Wheel/Weiser, LLC

With offices at:
665 Third Street, Suite 400
San Francisco, CA 94107
www.redwheelweiser.com

Library of Congress Cataloging-in-Publication Data

Short, Priscilla, 1969-

Thrifty green : ease up on energy, food, water, trash, transit,
stuff--and everybody wins / Priscilla Short.

p. cm.

Includes bibliographical references and index.

ISBN 978-1-57324-485-5 (alk. paper)

1. Energy conservation. 2. Renewable energy sources.
3. Power resources. I. Title.

TJ163.3.S487 2011

640--dc22   2011000821

Cover design by Jim Warner

Text design by ContentWorks, Inc.

Typeset in Goudy

Printed in the United States of America

TS

10 9 8 7 6 5 4 3 2 1

To Julie, who encouraged me
to do something creative.

Contents

Acknowledgments

MY HEARTFELT THANKS GO TO the people of Taos for welcoming me to my new home, particularly my builder, Charlie, and his wife Judit, my neighbors Joaquin and Agnes, Norbert and Shari, and especially Olive. Thanks also to the many friends whose stories became sidebars: you have all influenced my life more than you can know. And to my earliest and most lasting influences: my mother, who insisted that my sisters and I play outdoors regardless of weather, and my departed father, who was ahead of his time in terms of energy efficiency and architecture.

Thanks are also due to my agent, Krista Goering, who was open-minded enough to suggest this book; my editor, Caroline Pincus, who took a risk on a new author; and the staff at Red Wheel/Weiser for their professionalism and dedication to accuracy. Any factual errors or mistaken references are mine alone.

Above all, I would like to thank my husband, Jason, for giving me the time to write and words of encouragement when I needed them, and my daughter, Sarah, for lighting up my life.

Finally, to those who inquired about my book's progress over the past year (Margo, Kay, and all the others), I hope you enjoy it.

Introduction

Reality must take precedence over public relations, for nature cannot be fooled.

—Richard Feynman

I MAGINE A WORLD WITH NO pollution. Imagine fresh air and clean water and an abundance of natural resources. Imagine green fields of healthful foods, grazing animals with plenty of space, and all waste recycled productively instead of piling up in landfills. Imagine wild animals with room to roam, an ocean full of fish, and skies filled with birds.

Imagine also a life without stress, one where you have enough time to enjoy what the earth has to offer. Imagine a life lived in the slow lane, where you have time to visit with friends, cook your own meals, sleep eight (or more) hours a night, and put into practice all those things we are told we need to do for optimal health. Drink eight glasses of water each day. Floss. Exercise. Spend quality time with our children.

Now imagine that you are an integral part of the whole system, that your actions influence everything around you. Imagine living a life with zero impact on the earth. What would that look like? First and most important, you would consume no more energy than you produced. (If you wanted to set the bar higher, you could actually produce more energy than you consumed.) Your water source would be clean, and you would use no more of it than could be replenished naturally. Any water you returned to the system after using it would not be polluted or contaminated. You would eat food that had been grown locally and without the use of chemicals, so your eating habits wouldn't contribute to the pollution of the earth (or your body). You would compost your organic waste so it could be returned to the earth in a useful manner. You would not create any trash. Any waste items in your household would be reused to extend their life and reduce the number of new items you bought, or they would be burned for energy. When you had to travel, you would do so in such a way that you created no pollution, you used no more energy than you created, and your vehicle was not built at an excessive cost to the planet.

Does this sound idyllic? Or impossible? Who lives this way? Most of the earth's population does, although in conditions that are far from idyllic. Most of us in America have a long way to go to meet the zero-impact standard. It would be easy to condemn our wastefulness and predict that we will never be willing to sacrifice our standard of living enough to attain a zero-impact goal. You could extrapolate that line of thinking to predict the collapse of our ecosystems; our infrastructure; our energy, manufacturing, and agriculture industries, and—in a doom-and-gloom scenario—our society itself.

However, that would underestimate our famous ingenuity. This country is full of talented, creative, motivated citizens who are using new technology to come up with solutions to our environmental problems on a society-wide scale. You read about solar, wind, and other inventive sources of energy such as "clean coal" and synthetic natural gas all the time. You see ads for eco-friendly products for personal hygiene or to clean and decorate your house, "green" clothes to wear or sheets for the bed, and environmentally correct cars to drive. You can even take earth-friendly vacations to all points around the globe, or close to home at a local spa that will pamper you with products containing only natural ingredients.

The problem is that those "solutions" perpetuate the same way of life we have right now, and some of them aren't solutions at all. The real solution relies on neither technology breakthroughs nor buying yet more stuff, and it can be accomplished right now with no more investment than a willing attitude. What I am talking about is conservation.

Conservation seems to be making a comeback in the financial market–collapse hangover that we are collectively experiencing. Most of us are cutting back to save money, and it just happens to benefit the planet as well when we buy less stuff. If we're lucky, we will converge on a different way of life that is more satisfying than our recent spending binge, one that we will want to sustain in the future.

Actually, luck has less to do with it than making conscious choices, something I learned when, after two years of thinking about it and planning for it, I quit the stressful corporate job I had held for a decade, broke up with my boyfriend, sold my conventional house, and moved full-time to a small, solar-powered, straw bale house in the vast sagebrush outside of Taos, New Mexico. I had no central heating, no source of electricity beyond what the sun provided, and no water supply other than what I caught on the roof. Living on savings, disconnected from both mainstream America and the national power grid, I adjusted my life throughout the next four seasons to accommodate the quirks of the house and drastically downshifted the amount of electricity, water, and other resources I consumed.

Living in this kind of house meant I could see very clearly the effects of my consumption of energy and other resources on my quality of life. As I was also living on savings, I had to make choices that involved spending as little as possible as well. What I realized was that resource conservation and frugality were one and the same. With no TV, Internet, computer, washing machine or dryer, refrigerator, dishwasher, trash pickup, or snowplow service, I kept my food out back in a cooler, read by candlelight when the electricity cut out, stayed in when it snowed too much, and checked my email at Internet cafes. Yet I didn't feel deprived. I felt exhilarated. I wanted it to continue forever.

But by the end of a year, I had run out of money and had to return to Colorado, my former home, and take another corporate job. I expected it to feel different, but I didn't count on full-fledged culture shock. After only one year of unconventional living, I felt like a stranger in a setting that used to be familiar. The culture of a place wields a strong influence. Despite my best intentions, it wasn't quite so easy to be a conservationist when surrounded by mainstream American life's temptations to excess. Reality set in, and I slid back into some wasteful habits born of convenience. But not all of them. There are painless ways to conserve even on the grid, and I put my conscious decision-making skills into practice when deciding where to stick to my principles and where to let things slide.

Life for me now includes a husband (the boyfriend that I once broke up with) and the compromises of marriage, which also affect my decisions. So I adjust and readjust with each new scenario, keeping in mind the fundamental discovery I made off the grid in Taos: that what was good for me was also good for the planet, and that consuming less and conserving more helps us all.

A Different Way of Life

And the day came when the risk to remain tight in a bud was more painful than the risk it took to blossom.

—Anaïs Nin

TAOS IS A WELCOMING PLACE for souls in need of soothing. It's a beautiful area filled with funky, eclectic people. Ten years ago, I had a house built on two acres of land outside town in the middle of the high desert sagebrush. As the realtors like to say, it has 360-degree views. Translation: no trees. Further translation: big sky arching over the valley ringed by mountains. From my bedroom window, I could see Wheeler Peak, the highest mountain in New Mexico. Ten minutes west took me to the Rio Grande Gorge, where bald eagles nest in the winter and kayakers run the rapids in the summer. Fifteen minutes south, and I found myself in town. Thirty minutes east up a steep, winding road deposited me at the Taos Ski Valley. And an hour north brought me to the pristine Valle Vidal wilderness, home to the largest elk herd in the state.

It was the perfect place for a much-needed retreat from the stress of modern life. But what set the house apart from most vacation homes (I built it with the intention of only using it on weekends) and what set the wheels in motion for the most extraordinary year of my life, was the decision to have it be as inexpensive and environmentally friendly as possible. It was the culmination of a childhood spent largely outdoors in the mountains of Colorado and my father's lessons on energy-efficient architecture. He was a creative thinker in terms of home building and energy use, and my formative years were spent living in a house my dad had built himself during the last energy crisis in the '70s. I grew up on the phrases *put a sweater on* and *close the door, I'm not paying to heat the whole outdoors*. I learned about south-facing windows, sun angles, and insulation early on, and the term *R-value* entered my vocabulary before the age of ten.

R-Value

The R-value of a substance measures its thermal resistance. To state it differently, in the building industry, a material's R-value measures how efficient an insulator it is.

When dreaming of a second home in Taos, I researched the most far-out ideas I could find: straw bale construction, passive solar design, off-the-grid living, and self-sufficient renewable resources using a photovoltaic system and water catchment. The concepts were new and exciting, the perfect antidote to the bland sameness that characterized the rest of my life. When I was looking for land near Taos on which to build, I painted my vision for the real estate agent. She didn't bat an eye, nor did she think I was some kind of crackpot; she didn't even need me to define my vocabulary. That's when I knew Taos was the place for me.

Off the Grid

The grid refers to this country's regional networks of electrical generation, transmission, and distribution. They are interconnected and span the nation. The vast majority of Americans are connected to the grid, including some who actually generate their own power via solar panels or the like and sell it back to the utility companies. They are still connected. When I built my house in Taos, the grid was a mile from my land, and drawing a power line out was too expensive for my budget. So I built a house that generated all its power itself. It was not connected to the grid—also known as "off the grid" or sometimes "self-sustaining." I did not rely on public utilities to keep my lights on, nor did I have to pay utility bills, but I was therefore reliant on myself to use less energy than my system produced.

When I describe my house, I use words like *off-the-grid* (not connected to the national power grid); *active solar* (generates its own energy from the sun); *passive solar* (oriented to the south to optimize the heating potential of the sun); *straw bale* (has walls made of bales of straw); *water catchment* (catches water from rain and snow on the roof, drains it into a cistern and then pumps it back into the house and filters it for daily use); and *self-sustaining* (does not rely on anyone else to function). All six of those characteristics make it vastly different from the average American home, such as the one I formerly owned in Colorado, but it was exactly what I wanted. I wanted a retreat that was inexpensive to build, run, and maintain and one that I could lock and leave without worrying about it. I wanted a house with as small an ecological footprint as possible. When all was said and done, I wound up with a charming house that had no utility bills and a life lived in closer connection to my natural surroundings than I had since my childhood.

Ecological Footprint

An ecological footprint is the measure of our demand for the earth's resources as compared to the earth's capacity to regenerate those resources and absorb and neutralize the corresponding waste.[1] In other words, it represents our habits of consumption of energy and raw materials, plus our creation of waste products such as garbage and pollution. Individuals, companies, and countries can all have an ecological footprint. According to the latest calculations available from the United Nations, in 2009, humans on the planet collectively had an ecological footprint of 1.4, meaning it would take 1.4 earths to produce the resources we consume and to render our waste harmless.[2]

Electricity

If you are anywhere close to the grid, the cheapest option for power is to connect to it, assuming you think of cost in terms of dollars rather than cost to the planet. But if your state's energy comes from a dirty source such as coal (i.e., one that destroys ecosystems and creates pollution, as most states' energy does), then spending a few extra bucks on a personal solar energy system is the cheapest thing you can do for the planet in terms of resources. It is always a tradeoff.

But when you are a mile from the grid, as my house was when I built it, it is cheaper both in terms of dollars and environmental cost to use an active solar energy system and stay off the grid entirely. Pulling power out to my land from the grid would have required digging a mile-long trench (at two dollars per linear foot, plus seventy dollars an hour to backfill it), stringing the line out (at three dollars per linear foot), and installing a box and meter (eight hundred dollars), for a total cost of about thirty thousand dollars. By contrast, the active solar energy system cost roughly five thousand dollars. That was a simple decision. In my case, it was easy on the earth and on my wallet.

When you hear the term *solar energy*, you may think of banks of solar panels attached to someone's roof or soaking up the sun in an empty field somewhere. The collectors may look passive, but this is *active solar* energy. It requires an active mechanical system to collect sunlight and store it as electricity.

For a house the size of mine in Taos, the active solar energy system is called a photovoltaic system, named for the kind of photovoltaic (solar) panels I have mounted on a pole out back. The photovoltaic (PV for short) system consists of two solar panels to collect energy, four batteries to store it, and an inverter. The batteries are essentially car batteries, and the inverter is necessary to invert the electrical current from the direct current (DC) as it is stored in the batteries to the alternating current

(AC) needed by the electrical outlets. Virtually all electrical appliances in the United States require AC power.

When my builder, Charlie, walked me through the house upon my taking possession, he showed me how to use the inverter. It had three modes: on, off, and search. If I left it on, it consumed a tiny amount of electricity and made a constant buzzing sound, which is how I knew all my outlets and lights were powered. If I turned it off, it went silent and I had no current. If I left it in search mode, which was the most energy efficient, it sent out an intermittent pulse searching for anything that wanted to draw power. When it detected something, it kicked itself on. If I had actually kept a TV plugged in all the time so that it continuously drew a low level of power (called a phantom load), the inverter would stay on and slowly drain my batteries even if I wasn't watching TV.

What Charlie didn't mention was that certain items didn't draw enough power for the inverter to detect them and turn itself on. My cell phone was one example. When I plugged it in to charge it the first time, the inverter cycled on and off, confused and unable to decide whether something required power or not. It even did this if my charger was plugged in alone without the phone itself.

So, if I wanted to charge my cell phone, I had to manually turn the inverter on or turn on a light, which would keep the inverter on. That led to a search for the lowest-wattage bulb, something I had never paid attention to before, and subsequently to my decision to charge my phone only at night when the lights were already on so I wouldn't run the inverter unnecessarily. I had never before been this conscious of how my actions, however innocent seeming, affected the amount of electricity I used.

Charlie and Natural Builders

Charlie, also known as Carlos, runs a company called Natural Builders, which specializes in straw bale construction.[3] Charlie learned how to build self-sustaining houses in Mexico, where he spent two years building low-cost housing and learning while doing so, and where he met his wife, Judit. Eventually he and Judit landed in Taos to start a family. They live in an off-grid, straw bale house outside town that Charlie built himself using techniques the state of New Mexico considers "experimental," such as load-bearing straw bale walls. When I asked if he could use those techniques on my house out of a sense of environmental purity, he explained that legally, my house had to be inspected before he could issue me a certificate of occupancy, which I needed to insure it and pay property taxes. And the inspectors would expect my house to comply with state building codes. So no dice.

When designing the house, my architect, Joaquin, sized the PV system to accommodate its projected use. I told him I intended the house to be a weekend retreat—in other words, I wouldn't be leaving appliances on for longer than three days at a time—and my electrical needs were minimal anyway. Most of my large power needs, such as the stove and the tankless water heater, were fulfilled by propane. I required electricity for lights, the occasional kitchen appliance such as the toaster, the electric pump for water, and the refrigerator.

Joaquin

I met Joaquin just after I bought my land but before my road was built. He let me park on his land, right next to his adobe house, and leave my car there. He also gave me a tour of the first fully self-sustaining house I had ever seen. It was a work of art. Joaquin is a trained architect who came to New Mexico from Germany almost twenty years ago. His company, Zero E Design, specializes in eco-friendly and sustainable architecture.[4] When he first started, decades ago, he was so committed to his environmental principles that he wouldn't even build with concrete because of its environmental impact. His house on the mesa was built entirely out of adobe blocks including—impressively—a tightly sealed bathtub. Joaquin's work has outgrown the earlier passive solar/ adobe concept; the focus of his firm, in addition to these techniques, is now on ultralow-energy homes designed according to the European Passive House concept, a reduction of heating and cooling demand by an impressive 90 percent. He achieves this through the improved quality of the building shell alone without needing expensive solar mechanical systems.

When my house was built, we installed a small, under-counter electric refrigerator. The PV system was sized with a propane fridge in mind, but we couldn't find one of the right size in time, so I bought an inexpensive bar fridge instead. I purposefully bought a small one because I intended the house to be a vacation home, and I figured I would never have that much food there. In my daily life back in Colorado, I didn't have much food in the fridge anyway. Like a lot of single people, I kept my full-sized refrigerator full of alcohol, leftovers, condiments, and virtually nothing else, effectively paying the utility company to run an empty appliance. When I began living in my Taos home full-time, I asked Charlie how long the batteries would last with the electric refrigerator running. He said I would know the first time the power went out.

Water

In addition to being a mile from the grid, I was even farther from a county water source. The options when I built the house were to dig a well or to do water catchment. Wells cost eighteen dollars a foot at the time, and I had heard of people in the area drilling hundreds of feet for water. I chose water catchment because it cost less, and a cheap streak runs in my family.

Water catchment is simple: my water supply is caught on the roof and drained off into a three-thousand-gallon plastic cistern for storage and future use. My house has a slightly angled aluminum composite roof that drains into gutters that attach to a PVC pipe leading underground to the cistern. It is buried in a deep pit out back by the solar panels, beyond which lie the septic tank and leach field. To get the water into the house, Charlie installed an electric pump, my most consistent and necessary use of electricity. The pump is hooked to a pressure tank inside and kicks on automatically when the pressure drops to twenty pounds per square inch (psi). It runs for a few minutes, pumping water from the cistern inside until the pressure reaches forty psi. When I turn on a tap, water passes from the pressure tank through a filter before flowing out the faucet.

When Joaquin designed my house, he asked me questions about water that conventional architects don't ask, such as whether I wanted a flush or composting toilet. In the Taos area, nonstandard plumbing was common enough that his question to me wasn't unusual. For example, my neighbor Olive had an outhouse. If she had to go in the middle of the night, she grabbed a flashlight (or not, as the path was very familiar to her) and wended her way through the sagebrush.

A composting toilet uses no water and is thus a more conservation-minded choice than a flushable one. Nevertheless, I considered that my future guests would include my mother and her septuagenarian friends, who have been using standard toilets for decades and would be more comfortable with the familiar, and I opted for the flush toilet.

Another question was whether I wanted to install a gray water valve in the plumbing system. It would cost a little more, but if I didn't have it installed up front, I couldn't retrofit it in later.

There are two types of "used" water: gray and black. Black water is used water from the toilet, and gray water is used water from everything else, such as the water that runs down the drain when you take a shower or water from other sinks in the house. Gray water will contain soap or shampoo, food residue, and anything else you put down your sink whether you are aware of it or not. Municipal water authorities are starting to find traces of prescription medications, including endocrine disruptors (i.e., hormones) in their water supplies. If you limit what goes down your drains, gray water will mostly contain soap and traces of dirt or food. These materials don't affect plants, so gray water is a great environmental choice for watering them, either indoors or out.

Olive

I met Olive a year or so after I had built my house. I was still living in Colorado and using it as a weekend retreat for complete solitude. My two closest neighbors were unoccupied houses, each a mile away from me in either direction. One was a gorgeous, custom adobe home (Joaquin's), and the other a shack built on railroad ties.

One weekend I arrived at my house to find a note tacked to the doorframe. It had been fluttering there for weeks. The author wrote that she was interested in buying the shack and would like to talk to me about the area, which was situated between some mobile homes and a gravel pit. She signed it Olive and gave her phone number.

Olive went on to buy the land with the shack, which others would have considered a liability, given its deteriorating condition. But to Olive it was an asset. She lived in her Airstream trailer while she made the shack habitable by replacing the mouse-infested insulation, plastering the walls, pouring a concrete floor, installing a new front door and windows, building a porch, and putting a woodburning stove in a corner casement of bricks with a shelf for her cats to lie on. With the exception of the concrete floor, Olive did the work herself. It took a while, since she paid for it as she went, being unwilling to take on debt. Ultimately, she wound up with a cozy, artistic, unique little house.

However, as it still sat on railroad ties and had neither electricity nor running water, we continued to affectionately refer to it as "the shack."

Some houses are designed with indoor gray water planters, so that all gray water is diverted into them, where they simultaneously serve to nourish the plants and filter the water before it drains outside. The water is used twice before returning to the earth, a significant conservation feature.

In my case, the question was whether I wanted to be able to turn a valve and have either *all* used water flow into the septic tank, or only black water. In the latter case, gray water would come out a spigot on the exterior of the house where I could collect it and use it to water the garden. I said yes, I wanted one.

Initially, however, I opted to have both gray and black water flow into the septic system where it would be passively treated before seeping into the leach field to the north of the house.

Because I had a closed water system that included a septic tank, I had to be careful what I put down the kitchen sink. Besides, as I had no garbage disposal, I absolutely couldn't put food waste in it. But it also made me extremely cautious about disposing of chemicals, including household cleaning products. In my previous mainstream life, like most Americans, I didn't think twice about what I put down the drain until it got clogged.

In Taos, to be on the safe side, I cleaned my house with baking soda, white vinegar, Ivory soap, and nothing else. No bleach, no chemical cleaning products, nothing with ingredients I couldn't pronounce. This was partly out of concern for my health and the health of my surrounding environment but mostly because I didn't want to mess up my septic system. I figured that if I took care of it, I wouldn't have to pay to have it serviced or repaired as frequently. That cheap streak runs deep.

Another conservation decision we made was to install an on-demand water heater, also known as a tankless water heater. You can find these kinds of water heaters all over Europe, and they are starting to make an appearance in the United States as well. Instead of having a tank of water that is kept heated to a certain temperature at all times, which most conventional homes in America have, this kind of water heater draws in cold water (in my case from the pressure tank) and heats it on demand via propane. In other words, it heats water only when I turn on a hot water tap in a sink or the shower, so it uses propane only when I require it.

Zero Impact

One key conservation (and financial) benefit to my house is that when I am not there it uses no energy at all—no electricity and no propane. It has zero impact on the earth beyond simply existing in what would have been an empty field of sagebrush. No conventional house that I know of can make the same claim.

Yet there are definite idiosyncrasies to the self-contained water system of my house. One is that the tankless water heater will heat water only a certain number of degrees above ambient air temperature, roughly thirty degrees if I had to guess. During the summer, that isn't an issue. But during the winter, the season for steaming hot showers, I am forced to take lukewarm ones instead because the interior of the house is in the sixties, since I have no central heating.

Another, which I discovered accidentally, is what happens when I am taking a shower and the pump kicks on, meaning the pressure (and therefore the water level) in the pressure tank has dropped. The first time it happened, I wondered whether the flow of water out of the pressure tank to the shower would exceed the flow being pumped in. Out of precaution, I shut the water off and stood there a couple of minutes, soapy, wet, and shivering, until the pump switched off. Then I finished my shower.

The next time it happened, I tried a little experiment and continued my shower, wondering the whole time if I was going to be left with shampoo in my hair. As it turned out, the pump outpaced the shower, although toward the end the water pressure dropped, as did the temperature. My house is one big physics lesson.

I decided that in the future I would take a shower only when the pressure tank started off full, and I would limit my time so I would finish before the pump kicked on. Until I moved off the grid, I had never had to act so conscientiously or plan water use so carefully.

The most prominent characteristic that I still must be aware of, though, is that there is a finite water supply for all my water uses. I can walk out back and look at it. At least, I can look at the opaque lid of the cistern, but I can't tell how much water is in it. Uncertainty forces me to conserve water out of prudence. I never know when I might run out.

Water is the resource whose conservation I worry about most in my house (and in our country). I can live without electricity, and I can live without propane, but I can't live without water. Except that electricity and water are linked in my setup. The pump that pumps water from the cistern outside to the pressure tank inside is electric. If I run out of electricity, I can't run the pump. Therefore, if I run out of electricity, I run out of water except for what remains in the pressure tank. I have to conserve this extremely limited amount (twenty gallons or less) until the batteries recharge and I can run the pump again.

Heat

When I was in college, I took Astronomy 101 because we needed a lab science to graduate and my roommate coerced me into taking it with her. It wound up being one of my favorite courses, largely because the professor was brilliant, if a little nutty. (One day she brought her guitar and sang us the "Moon Song" she had written in 1969 when our astronauts took their first lunar steps.)

The lab portion of the class was conducted mostly gazing upward from the roof of the science center, which became colder and colder as autumn progressed. But one of the most interesting "lab experiments" we did was a semester-long project on sun motion. (Technically, it's earth motion relative to the sun.) The professor handed out copies of our college's skyline as seen when facing west while standing on the building's roof. At four points during the semester we were supposed to climb up there and record, via drawing, the location and time of the sunset. I already knew that the sun rises in the east, swings around to the south during the course of the day, and sets in the west, but this was a visually instructive lesson on how the sun sets more to the northwest the closer it is to the summer solstice, and more to the southwest in the dead of winter. It also demonstrated the rate at which days shorten as winter approaches. If we had done a similar experiment with sunrise, we would have seen several minutes lopped off either end of the day during the waning weeks of the year.

After college, in Taos, I replicated the assignment and discovered that the sun sets far south of Wheeler Peak in midwinter and far north of it midsummer, which affected which windows the sun shone through in each season.

The angle of the sun also changes throughout the year. During the summer, it is high overhead, and in the winter it is low enough to get in your eyes at two in the afternoon. What this meant for my house in Taos was that the sun penetrated the south-facing windows to a depth of twelve feet at the winter solstice, and then retreated to a depth of four inches at the summer solstice. In practical terms, it meant I had to drape a blanket over the piano in the far reaches of the room so the winter sun wouldn't fade the wood.

My house is passive solar, which means it heats and cools itself with no help from energy sources other than the sun. A passive solar house takes advantage of the changing location and angle of the sun, the goal being to welcome the sun for its free heat in the winter, but to keep it out in the summer. The first step is to orient the house properly. If you want the sun to come in and warm the house, which I did, you make sure your windows are mostly on the south side, which Joaquin did. (If you don't—for example, if you live in the Deep South and prefer to keep the sun out of your house at all times—then put them on the north side.) Windows on the east side will allow in gentle morning sun, south-facing ones admit light all day, and windows on the west will let in hot afternoon sun. As my dad used to say, "A window is a hole in the wall that lets light in and heat out." I have a small amendment: it lets heat in too, particularly during the winter when the sun is lower in the sky. Free heat from a clean source, the best kind.

After orienting a passive solar house properly, the second step is to make sure it contains thermal mass and quality insulation. Thermal mass is material in the house with a high capacity to store heat within itself. Insulation is material used to reduce the rate of heat transfer, such as from inside to outside, for example. The two work together in a passive solar house.

In my case, the thermal mass came in the form of a concrete slab, which itself did double duty as both foundation and floor material. Joaquin used several cost-saving methods such as this when designing the house. Since I didn't require a basement, I could have a slab foundation, which could easily be stained an attractive color and used as the floor.

During the summer, when the sun barely penetrated the south-facing windows, the concrete floor stayed blissfully cool under my bare feet. In the depths of winter, the sun poured through the windows to heat the floor all day. After sunset, the concrete slab slowly released its stored heat back into the room, the job of thermal mass. Good wall insulation kept the heat in the house, except for the bit that went out the windows. ("A window is a hole in the wall that lets light in and heat out." You can't escape it.) For my house, bales of straw provided both insulation and wall material, another cost savings.[5]

This style of building not only lends itself aesthetically to southwestern-style architecture, but is also a brilliant and simple way to have a temperate house with no heating or air conditioning systems. That means no energy expended and no bills to pay—and in the typical

Straw Bale Building

When I was researching passive solar homes, I came across the straw bale building idea. Straw bale is exactly what it sounds like: bales of straw. Eighteen inches wide and tied with string or wire, they are highly insulative because of the thousands of tiny air pockets between the straws. They are also relatively fireproof, according to tests done by the state of New Mexico and Canada. The biggest enemy of straw bale is water, which is why the first layer of bales is wrapped in a moisture barrier.

When building, you stack the bales the way you would bricks and pin each course with bamboo or rebar. According to the New Mexico state building code, you must build a post-and-beam structure to bear the weight of the roof (because the bales tend to settle) and use straw bales only as infill. But they make dandy wall material and deep-set windowsills characteristic of southwestern-style architecture, and you can finish them however you like.

conventional house not designed to make optimal use of sun motion, those can be some hefty bills.

My house does not have central heating, which saves money in multiple ways: there is no furnace to buy, maintain, run, or replace. It also has no air-conditioning: cross breezes will suffice. Passive solar design is effective and inexpensive.

One caveat, though, is that you have to live in a sunny climate to have a fully passive solar house. But even if you live in a cloudy area, you can still put passive solar principles into action and at least reduce your utility bills, if you can't eliminate them entirely.

Furthermore, you can't control the temperature in a passive solar house as precisely as you can with a thermostat. The temperature in my house on a cloudy winter day stays around sixty degrees. If I wanted it to be warmer than that, I needed a source of backup heat. Yet that still didn't need to mean a furnace and heating ducts. For me, it meant a woodburning stove. It could also mean strategically placed space heaters, turned on only when needed. Or it could mean a pair of wool socks and a mug of cocoa.

Every decision made while building my house in Taos—whether it had to do with energy for appliances, water, or heating and cooling—was made with an eye toward cost savings and environmental impact. The benefits were many, and the tradeoff was only that I had to pay conscious attention to resource usage. In the end, that turned out to be a benefit as well.

The Grand Vision

I have a plan for my house in Taos that I call the Grand Vision. The house itself is still the same 688-square-foot box with minimal landscaping that it was a decade ago when I had it designed. I like to think big, but I'm a little slow on implementation. Life gets in the way sometimes.

The Grand Vision includes creating outdoor rooms to stay better connected with Nature. It involves building a garden wall on the east side and planting flowers and plants within the enclosed space to attract hummingbirds and butterflies. Maybe it will have a nice table and chairs so I can take my breakfast outdoors comfortably. On the west side of the house, I will replace the impressively named but meagerly executed Sunset Terrace. Currently it consists of concrete pavers set directly on the ground so I can have a place to put my lawn chairs. I'd like to make it more permanent and to have a low wall for visual definition and more plants.

Nature with a Capital *N*

I always think of Nature as a person. She is generous and forgiving, but only up to a point. Mess with her too much, and she will show you who is boss. Out of a healthy sense of respect, I refer to her as *Nature* rather than *nature*.

To the south, I want to plant a garden of hardy plants. I have already tried this four times but have never been able to stick around long enough to give the plants the water they need to set deep enough roots for regeneration. When I leave, rabbits eat everything down to the ground.

The Grand Vision also calls for growing some of my own food; I intend to build a greenhouse so the fruits and vegetables can thrive in a rabbit-proof setting. It will be a passive solar structure with water catchment to provide a replenishable water source and enough sun for tropical plants. My idea of heaven is being able to grow my own avocados.

There will be a garage to house my car during snow-storms, perhaps with extra sleeping quarters on top. This may have a south-facing living roof where I could grow strawberries.

As for the rest of my land—all two acres of it—I would like to restore it to its original high-desert glory so it can be an oasis of indigenous plants that may eventually spread their way through the sagebrush and retake their ancestral home.

Invasive Plants

Sagebrush is an invasive plant in this part of New Mexico. The mesa used to be a prairie containing multiple types of grass, only two of which are now found in any real quantity. Overgrazing caused the grasses to disappear and gave the sagebrush the opportunity to take over.

The Grand Vision is mostly about connecting with the earth: growing food, restoring the landscape, or just appreciating its beauty. The way I lived in my straw bale house during my year off the grid serves as a blueprint for conscientious decision making in the future for me, and perhaps for all of us.

Bringing the Grand Vision to the Grid

When I ran out of savings and moved back to mainstream America to get married and take another corporate job, I knew I would be compromising some of my environmental ideals. It's too hard to swim against the current. But I vowed I would examine every aspect of energy and resource use in my on-grid life and consciously choose where to compromise and where to stick to my off-grid principles. It wound up being easier than

I thought because a lot of my conservation efforts had become ingrained from a full year of practice.

Back in Colorado, my husband and I bought a small house—a conscious decision, as opposed to buying one with a view or granite countertops or whatever else realtors like to put in listings. Living in a small house brings all kinds of costs down. We have few electric needs in general, and we keep them low by leaving lights off and owning small appliances that we run infrequently. Some of the biggest changes for me come in actually having appliances to run, infrequently or not.

The most significant compromises I make these days have come about because we had a baby. We do orders of magnitude more laundry these days than I ever did living solo off the grid. We also use disposable diapers, a decision we made after much conscience-wrenching back-and-forthing.

The decisions are all connected and sometimes contradictory, although we like to think that we conserve more than the average American household. On the one

If you focus on saving water and I concentrate on saving electricity, it can have the same result as if we both saved a little of both. All it takes is a few conscious choices on the part of each individual to collectively make a big impact.

hand, we use more water by doing more laundry. But we use less water by using disposable diapers. Yet we create more garbage. Which is offset by our compost heap and recycling ethic and by the fact that I cook as many fresh meals as I did off the grid. I buy fresh produce and meat, which subsequently requires less packaging. But I do have to shop more often, which would entail more driving except that we deliberately chose to live in a small town where we can walk most places, including the grocery store, even with the baby.

When my car died, we chose not to replace it and instead decided to live as a one-car family for a while. My husband commutes, sometimes by car and other times by bus, depending on the location of the job.

Living in a small house also means that we have limited space in which to store our stuff, so we have stopped buying stuff. We have consciously decided to make our lives about experiences rather than the accumulation of stuff. It's good for the environment and good for our bank account. It's all connected.

We're all connected too on this planet: neighbors, countries, animals, plants, ecosystems. What each of us chooses to do ultimately affects us all. The good news is that the effects can be positive and not everybody has to do everything. If you focus on saving water and I concentrate on saving electricity, it can have the same result as if we both saved a little of both. If you recycle everything and I always take public transportation, that has a positive result as well. All it takes is a few conscious choices on the part of each individual to collectively make a big impact. Small steps are a start, but it's good to think big. Even if you accomplish only half of what you intend, it's still much more than if you had planned nothing at all.

I have a Grand Vision for this country too. It involves no pollution from cars and little if any from factories. I envision people growing at least some of their own food to stay in touch with how it is produced and obtaining the rest from local farmers and ranchers. In my fantasy, nobody lives in a huge house on a small lot but rather the reverse: everyone has a yard or access to open space if they live in big cities. Cities have parks and trees and songbirds, and people walk or bike to work to maintain their health. There is adequate, inexpensive public transportation for inclement weather, and people use it instead of owning cars. Pollution is down, contact with Nature is up, and everyone is healthier, happier, and less stressed. Everyone makes conscious choices to practice conservation, and no one minds.

This book includes stories of people making conscious decisions large and small for a variety of reasons. They may be motivated by saving money, helping the environment, or something else entirely, but the result is the same. It also provides examples of different—yet entirely civilized—ways of life in other countries that result in the conservation of the planet's resources.

None of these examples is of people sacrificing to the point of deprivation. Neither does this book depict eco-minded stunts that real people can't achieve and even the stuntmen can't sustain. Nor do I advocate spending money on products just because they are marketed as "green." There is another way to achieve a smaller ecological footprint. It requires a wholesale mind shift and the embracing of a different way of life, and it's something we all can do.

The Earth's Resources

In the loosest sense, the earth has two types of resources: nonrenewable and renewable. We as a nation have been rapidly consuming the earth's nonrenewable resources ever since the Industrial Revolution. These include petroleum products such as oil and gasoline, other fossil fuels such as coal and natural gas, minerals and metals that are extracted from the earth usually at a great environmental cost, and even the land itself. As Will Rogers once quipped, "Land is the one thing they aren't making any more of." Nonrenewable resources can all be classified that way: things they aren't making any more of. When they're gone, they're gone.

Renewable resources include anything we use that can be replenished: water, forests, agriculture, resources from the sea such as fish or waves (potentially useful in generating energy), wind, and sunshine. Yet just because a resource can be replenished doesn't mean it can't be overtaxed. We are certainly capable of cutting down enough trees that they can't grow back into the dense forests they once were. We are currently in the process of taking so many fish from the ocean that they can't reproduce fast enough to keep up with our appetite. While these resources may be renewable, they are still subject to supply-and-demand laws and may wind up diminished to the point of annihilation.

When I refer to resources in this book, I am talking about all of these—renewable, nonrenewable, clean (e.g., sunshine), and dirty (e.g., coal). They are all necessary to our way of life and are thus all precious.

2

Heat

Don't fight forces, use them.

—R. Buckminster Fuller

ONE FRIGID JANUARY SHORTLY AFTER building my house in Taos, I hosted a girls' weekend for some friends. The ground was frozen, and snow lingered in shady spots and low points on the road where cold air collected. The temperature wasn't forecasted to rise above twenty degrees, although the sun was shining brightly. It is a paradox in this climate that sunny days in winter can be significantly colder than cloudy ones. But clouds hold heat over the earth's surface, and clear skies—especially at night—allow the warmest air to rise, cool, and become useless.

The morning was cold and sunny when my friends decided to go for a run. Triathletes all, they couldn't afford to skip a day of training for the upcoming season. They invited me to come with them, even suggesting that I ride my bike to keep up since I don't run. Ever. I passed, preferring some downtime. I watched as they set off and then retired to the window bench under my south-facing windows to relax and read a book.

Within ten minutes of bright sun bearing down on me, I needed to strip off my sweater, followed by my wool socks, and then my fleece pants, and more. There are no neighbors within binocular distance to ogle me, but even so I modestly changed into shorts and a tank top after another ten minutes had passed and I continued to heat up. By the time my friends returned, I lay comfortably sweating on the cushions in full sunshine. They were pink-cheeked and sniffled through chilly noses, despite having had their blood pumping for nearly an hour. Meanwhile, having expended no energy whatsoever, I had stayed almost too warm.

When I researched designs for my house in Taos, keeping it warm while expending no energy whatsoever was my goal. Most modern "green" construction, by contrast, seeks only to minimize the energy consumed for heating. That's a worthy goal, but I wanted to eliminate it, mostly because I am too cheap to pay utility bills if I don't have to.[6]

The Taos climate is one of extremes, and houses must be built to accommodate them. Winter nights are routinely below freezing and frequently sub-zero. Summers bring long stretches of temperatures above ninety degrees. It is a testament to human evolution that we are capable of withstanding both extremes, even without modern conveniences. The Taos Pueblo, in fact, has been continuously occupied for over a thousand years, more than four times as long as the United States has existed.

Even before the Taos Pueblo, ancient peoples settled in other parts of New Mexico. The Ancestral Pueblo People, from whom the Taos Pueblo tribe are descended, built a settlement in what is now Bandelier National Monument.[7]

These settlements took advantage of New Mexico's relentlessly sunny climate to use passive solar principles for heating and cooling. They probably didn't call it that, just as they doubtless didn't weigh the thermal advantages of adobe as a building material. They simply took advantage of what was at hand and worked in concert with Nature. As anyone who has ever tried to divert a stream knows, it is easier to work with Nature than against her.

If you live in a forest, you tend to build your shelter from wood, as the Native Americans of the Pacific Northwest did. If your home sits on a belt of limestone, you build stone walls that last for centuries, as they have in the Cotswolds in England. If your soil is a thick clay, as it is in rural Mali, you sculpt it into mud brick structures and replaster them annually. And if you are the Ancestral Pueblo People, you notice that the snow melts on one half of your canyon long before it melts on the other, and you dig caves into the soft cliff walls on that side and stack mud bricks into houses in front of them to stay warm in the winter.

Making use of indigenous materials when building a house is the most environmentally friendly approach you can take. (It also produces architecture unique to your

Bandelier National Monument

Bandelier National Monument is a high-altitude wilderness that is home to cliff dwellings and other archeological ruins of the Ancestral Pueblo People. Located near Los Alamos in northern New Mexico, its climate is arid and its geography mountainous high desert. As with the rest of the state, the sun is a prominent fixture in the sky the majority of the year. Rain, if it falls at all, comes sporadically in summer afternoon thundershowers, and winter snowfall is minimal.

Although there is evidence of over ten thousand years of human habitation in the area, the Ancestral Pueblo People created permanent settlements not quite a thousand years ago and abandoned them four hundred years later. Visitors to the national monument can take a paved trail along Frijoles Creek to the most striking of the ruins: the cliff dwellings known as Long House and a ceremonial kiva called Alcove House.

On a temperate day late one December, a friend and I walked through the ruins along the canyon floor on our way to the cliff dwellings. Because it was winter, we had worn several thermal layers (long underwear, sweaters, down jackets, hats, and gloves), for which we were grateful as the shady trail threaded its way through the tall ponderosa pines and snow clinging to the banks of the creek. But the moment we burst out of the trees into bright sunshine, the temperature changed, and we shed our jackets.

By the time we reached the cliff face where the dwellings had been carved out of volcanic tuff, we were in our bottommost layers. Long House is located on the south-facing wall of the cliff where it receives sunshine for the entire day during winter. The Ancestral Pueblo People, needing a heat source, took advantage of the solar gain (i.e., heat from the sun) to heat their homes during the day with minimal extra fuel or work. In a labor-intensive life, eliminating any work is important. In a cold climate, free heat is invaluable.

locale, versus the bland uniformity of America's creeping suburbs.) Coming in at a close second is taking advantage of the natural energy resources provided by your climate and geography. To utilize them, you have to pay attention to your surroundings as the Ancestral Pueblo People did. But these days we suffer from a condition I call "overdomestication," which is characterized by being oblivious to Nature despite living in it.

Quick: What phase of the moon are we in? Is it waxing or waning? What time is sunrise, and where does the sun come up relative to your local landmarks? What direction does the wind come from, and does its intensity change throughout the day? Can you locate north without a compass? What animals migrate to, from, or through where you live? If you live by the ocean, do you know when high and low tide occur? How high and low do they get? What seasonal produce is your area known for? What kinds of animals do you see most often near where you live? What month does spring come and how can you tell? By blossoming trees, migrating songbirds, chinook winds?

If you can't answer these questions, you might suffer from overdomestication.[8] And if that's the case, you probably live in a house that requires you to turn on the furnace to warm up and the air-conditioner to cool off. You are working against Nature, not with her, and that is costing you money every month in the form of utility bills.[9] It also costs our planet by consuming more nonrenewable resources than necessary. (Unless you heat your home with a renewable source, in which case, good for you.)

How Warm Do You Need to Be?

On a typical midwinter day at my house in Taos, the mountains on the east side of the mesa delay sunrise until almost 7:30 a.m. Even then, the sun doesn't actually come in the bedroom window to strike my face and wake me up because the bathroom bump-out blocks it from November until February. Instead, I wake up slowly when the sky becomes light, soaking in a state of half sleep. Clocks had no place in my year off the grid, just as they are unnecessary in the natural world. Once awake, I linger in bed until the sun brightens up the living room and brings back the warmth that fled from the house overnight. The temperature in my house dips to fifty degrees after sunset and stabilizes there until morning thanks to the straw bale walls. Without another source of heat besides the sun, I stay warm beneath a down comforter until it's time to throw it off and confront the chilly morning air, which I do in the bathroom where the sun's rays warm my body through an east-facing window as I splash cold water on my face.

In reality, I do have another source of heat: a woodburning stove. It does a reasonable job on a winter night of warming the house to about sixty degrees, which is better than fifty, but that's only if I keep the fire stoked and roaring. If you have ever spent the weekend camping out, you know that there is nothing like the friendly crackle of a campfire blaze for warmth and camaraderie. It's a pleasant diversion for an evening to poke the fire and throw more logs on when it dwindles. Like most dreamers, I am a firewatcher and enjoy contemplating the flames as they dance.

The Effectiveness of Woodburning Stoves

Colorado has a system of backcountry huts that are accessible in winter only by nonmotorized methods. To reach them, you must ski or snowshoe several miles into the forest through scenery unspoiled by human activity. The "huts" themselves are actually large log cabins, some of them quite grand, but all of them rustic in that they are completely off the grid.

Solar panels provide the minimal electricity used by the light bulbs. Woodburning stoves provide heat and cooking facilities. The huts come stocked with pots and pans for cooking but also for gathering snow to melt for water. Some huts have pumps; most do not. There are composting toilets in outbuildings since there is no running water. All of them have beautiful views from their decks. And at least one of them, called Vance's Cabin, has a sauna.

One winter I visited Vance's Cabin with a group of friends during a severe cold snap. Colorado winters are usually mild, with daytime temperatures in the forties and nighttime temps maybe going down to the twenties. During this cold snap, though, daytime highs were in the teens and nighttime lows dropped below zero.

While my friends were game for an adventure, my colleagues at work in Colorado Springs thought we were nuts. As we left the office that Friday, they worried we wouldn't be warm enough and headed off to their centrally heated homes with vaulted ceilings and large banks of west-facing windows. We headed into the high country where it was even colder than Colorado Springs.

The next day, we snowshoed our way three miles into the backcountry, working up a sweat, to reach Vance's Cabin by midday. The first order of business was setting up shop, which involved claiming bed space for our sleeping bags, chopping wood and building a fire in the woodburning stove, gathering snow to augment the water supply left by the previous occupants, and preparing food for dinner. The chores were the same that any pioneer family in the 1800s faced, the kind of labor that will work up an appetite in addition to a sweat, and we tucked into dinner with relish.

After dinner, we played cards and stoked the fire until we were so hot we had to strip down to t-shirts. Then somebody had the brilliant idea of getting in the sauna. Vance's Cabin's sauna is equipped with its own woodburning stove, so we built a fire there too and kept feeding it logs until it pumped out more heat than I could handle. In a pair of shorts and a tank top, ten minutes was all I could take before I gave up and went outside into the night to thrust my hands into a snowbank to cool down.

Back at the office on Monday, my coworkers were surprised to learn that I had stayed warmer than they had.

But keeping a fire going every night as a heat source is something else entirely. It distracts from my other activities as it periodically forces me off the couch and out from under the comforter I have wrapped around me to keep everything but my fingers warm while I read my book.

When I lived on the grid before Taos, if I became cold, I turned up the thermostat and diligently paid my utility bill each month. In Taos, I had no thermostat. Also no bill. Instead, I adjusted my idea of warmth ten degrees downward and paid strict attention to anything having to do with heat loss. I never left the front door open. I wore heavy sweaters and wool socks indoors at night. I drank mug after mug of hot tea. And I sat under my down comforter when I needed an extra layer. The house may have been colder than any on-grid house I had ever lived in, but that was because it required me to expend my own energy to heat it. My biggest self-revelation in Taos was that I would rather be cold than exert myself, and I quit building fires out of sheer laziness. I got tired of interrupting my reading every half hour to see whether the logs were burning evenly or, worse, to bring more wood in from outside if it was running low.

But there was another reason as well. Building a fire every night uses quite a bit of wood. Paying for half a cord of wood each winter is probably cheaper than six months of utility bills, but it shocked me to see how quickly the logs went up in smoke. As the one who carried them from the woodpile outdoors to the metal container indoors and the one who fed them one by one to the stove, I silently willed each log to burn a long time so I could minimize my trips outside to fetch more.

If you are physically involved in producing the heat for your house, you very quickly decide to use less heat.

(If you are several steps removed from your heat source and you can afford to pay the heating bill, only your conscience will prevent you from cranking the thermostat.) Hauling firewood may be good exercise, but it's no fun when it's fifteen degrees and snowing outside. Faced with the tradeoff of expending energy (my own and the planet's) to stay warm versus enduring a little cold, I decided that sitting under a down comforter was just as good as a nightly fire, or even better. It cost me nothing either in terms of dollars or labor, and it allowed me to read without interference.

Granted, I have a high tolerance for suffering, so this is a deal I was willing to make. Despite the fact that I love being warm on a cold night, once I moved off the grid I had to change both my definition of warmth and the mechanism for achieving it. These are the two parts of the equation to keep in mind when figuring out a way to expend less energy (and therefore money) in a conventional house. First, how warm do you really need to be? And second, where does your heat come from?

It was easy to be smug about not needing to be as warm as my on-grid friends when I didn't have the option of turning up the thermostat. I never had to challenge my willpower. I was never tempted, so I couldn't give in. Except, notably, when I visited those friends in their on-grid houses. Then I would afford myself the luxury of not wearing a wool sweater indoors. I didn't need to huddle under a blanket, and sometimes I went so far as to take a hot shower to warm up—something I also couldn't do off the grid but used to do routinely before I moved to Taos.

However, after living off the grid for a month or two, I recognized that being able to sit around in your shirtsleeves in seventy-degree temperatures indoors in the middle of winter was a luxury. It is neither a necessity nor a right. Energy has been cheap for long enough in the United States that we have collectively forgotten what it was like to live without it. Once you become accustomed to something, you tend to think of it as the norm and to feel entitled to it, like a heated home in a cold climate.

Life without Heat

In 2001, I went trekking in Nepal. It was April, a month that brings volatile weather to the Rocky Mountains in the United States and, apparently, similar weather to the Himalayas. After a few days of mild weather on the trek, it snowed several feet, and nighttime temperatures plummeted. The teahouses where we stayed had thin plywood walls with no insulation. The only source of heat came from a stove in the common room where they burned yak dung, which smells exactly as you imagine it might. There was no central heat, no furnace, no truck delivering heating oil (and no roads on which to drive one), and even scant wood to burn. The Nepalese burned the one fuel they had in plenty. Even with a fire going downstairs, the upstairs bedrooms were cold. We slept fully clothed in down sleeping bags, clutching bottles of boiled water that would serve as our drinking water the next day. It's an existence lived close to the bone, but rather than making me long for the comforts of home, I felt more alive than I had in years. The Nepalese, of course, have no other practical options. For them, life without heat is normal.

After only a scant few weeks off the grid, low indoor temperatures became normal for me; I had already adjusted to the point where I didn't feel uncomfortably cold at night with no fire going. I didn't even realize it until I invited some girlfriends down for a visit from Colorado in early November. They all kept their jackets on indoors until one of them finally asked me to build a fire. Wearing only a sweater, I hadn't thought it was cold. After I built the fire, I couldn't sit next to it without overheating.

Acclimating to a downward shift in temperatures takes very little time, in case you are considering turning down your thermostat, a tried-and-true way to save energy and money. All it takes is a change in attitude and a redefinition of how warm you really need to be. But this is harder than it sounds when it is so easy and costs so little to keep the thermostat high. My own resolve was tested when I moved back on the grid into a house that was built in 1947. It was quite a reality check. I learned a lot from living off the grid, but I learned even more by subsequently moving back on. Like a lot of houses built in 1947, ours had no insulation—as in zip, zero, none whatsoever. We bought it because my husband and I liked the neighborhood, and I started singing a less self-righteous tune. Our house faces southwest, which is less optimal than facing south. It overheats in the summer and is frigid in the winter. We are in the process of remedying this, and I have discovered that retrofitting a house to be greener is much harder than starting from scratch.

In the meantime, I have begun turning the heat up at night. My tolerance for cold seems to reside off the grid in Taos. Back in the mainstream where I have a thermostat, it is too easy to push up the lever ever so slightly to warm up. Energy is still cheap, our utility bills are low, and we have an income to pay them, which I also lacked in Taos.

Initially this made me feel wasteful and guilty until I decided to change my attitude again. There was no way I was going to match my off-grid ecological footprint when living in a conventional house, so I decided to conserve where I reasonably could to balance out the more wasteful aspects of my life on-grid. I also decided the conservation habits I learned in Taos could be painlessly applied with decent results on-grid.

To start, I take advantage of solar gain for free heat whenever I can, even though our house is not quite oriented properly. On all sunny days—and there are plenty during an average Colorado winter—I completely turn off the heat during the day and let the sun keep our house warm. Since the house is small, it works well enough. The kitchen and back bedroom get a little cool, so I spend my time in the sun-filled living room. Once the sun goes down, I shut all the shades and turn the heat back on.

It always surprises me to walk through my neighborhood on a sunny winter day and see homes with their shades pulled down to keep the sun out. Maybe my neighbors are worried their carpets will fade, or maybe they don't realize the power of passive solar principles, but they are expending energy and spending money unnecessarily. Instead of working with Nature to heat their houses in a clean, free manner, they are paying to do battle with her. There are other options.

My other strategy at night is to cook dinner at home. Reheating in the microwave doesn't count. Turning the oven on warms the kitchen as effectively as the furnace, and we eat well to boot. Any solution that involves one action (or appliance or whatever) doing double duty is a

Turn It Down or Turn It Off?

If you live in a house that was built in the past twenty years, it is probably better to turn your heat down than off or invest in a programmable thermostat that will do it for you, since it takes more energy to bring the temperature up from a cold point than to consistently maintain a cool one. Your house probably has good insulation and a thermostat that (presumably) can be found in a central location. In our house, this isn't the case. The thermostat is located near the kitchen, which is on the north side of the house. Couple that with no insulation, and our kitchen is always cold in the winter. If the heat is on, even if it is set to a low temperature, the location of the thermostat guarantees that the furnace will kick on more frequently than necessary to heat the rest of the house. Because I don't need it on when I spend my afternoons in the warm living room, I turn the heat all the way off and expend no energy unnecessarily.

form of conservation. It's all connected, and all the small, conscious choices add up to big results.

Using less energy to heat your home will require a shift in thinking. If you are in the market to buy, build, or rent a new place to live, it's time to stop thinking in terms of window views or street-facing houses, and replace that thinking with a knowledge of north, south, east, and west. The goal is to find a new home that faces south.

You will find plenty of space in books and magazines devoted to building a new house using passive solar and other environmental systems, but building a brand new house always comes with an ecological cost unless you are

> *All the small, conscious choices add
> up to big results.*

dedicated enough to use 100 percent locally scrounged salvage material. An especially bad idea is bulldozing your house and building a new one—the antithesis of conservation.[10] If you rent, you have an easier time: simply move to a place with as many energy conservation and passive solar principles implemented as possible. Landlords don't charge extra for those. Usually they charge extra for views, and unless the view is to the south, this can work in your favor.

If you are lucky, you already live in a house that is oriented toward the south to take advantage of solar gain. Most existing homes weren't laid out that way, and most people don't take that into consideration when buying a house. Even I didn't when I moved back on the grid, despite my addiction to sunshine and my husband's and my commitment to saving energy and money. We bought ours for the quiet, tree-lined streets, and because of our wonderful neighbors. You can't buy good neighbors.

So what else can the owner of an existing home do beyond turning the heat down?

As has been amply documented, when retrofitting an existing house to use less energy for heat, the first, best, and in some cases, only step is to insulate, insulate, insulate. We started with the attic, and my self-righteous attitude took another hit. I wanted to find someone who would blow cellulose up there since it is comprised of 80 percent postconsumer recycled newspaper that has been treated to resist fire and mold. As ecologically sensitive insulation goes, it's not as good as straw bale, but it is better than fiberglass or

Natural Air-Conditioning

Most homes in Colorado Springs, where I lived for many years, do not have air-conditioning if they were built before the huge influx of immigrants from other parts of the country. Colorado Springs has reliable and sometimes quite fierce winds that are the product of its location at the place where the plains meet the mountains. All you need to cool your house in the summer is to open the windows on the east and west sides to take advantage of perpetual cross breezes. (Work with Nature, not against her.)

Also, the mountains to the west of the city dependably produce clouds and thundershowers every summer afternoon. There's nothing like a good rainstorm to cool temperatures down by twenty degrees and wash everything clean for the evening. Taos, with mountains to the east, has summer monsoon showers as well.

Coincidentally, as Colorado Springs' population increased in the late 1990s, a drought descended and the thundershowers disappeared. Then everyone started building homes with air-conditioners. Around this time, I bought a townhouse on the west side of town and opted against paying for an air-conditioner. Instead, I chose a unit with southern exposure and east-west windows. My house was well lit, temperate, cheerful, full of thriving plants, and heated and cooled almost for free. It was also difficult to sell when the time came, because most people don't think this way and so the benefits were lost on potential buyers. When I built the house in Taos, I decided never to sell it, which freed me to build it to my specifications rather than society's.

other conventional options. But when I called around in October 2009 after the first of four snowstorms that month, the quickest option was a contractor who could come the next day and spray in twelve inches of loose-fill fiberglass. That was the first of our on-grid compromises.

The modern tradeoff seems to be between time and money. With little time, we took the first and easiest solution that came along and threw some money at it. The fiberglass cost $280 after a $70 rebate from our utility company. We would have had him do the walls and floor too, but he only took cash, and ours was spoken for until the next paycheck.

I still feel guilty, though, for not making more of an effort to find what I wanted. (I also wish that "green" insulation options were more mainstream and therefore more readily available so I wouldn't have to make an effort.) I dislike compromising out of convenience, because once you start, it is easy to convince yourself that you really had no choice. You always have a choice, even if you don't always have the mental fortitude to make it.

On the plus side, the attic insulation has somewhat helped keep heat in the house. Now the furnace doesn't cycle on as often even if we have the thermostat turned up, so in one sense we are saving energy.

Insulation is a cost- and energy-efficient solution, but be careful that you don't jump too quickly on the green bandwagon without doing your homework. Technological advances being what they are, companies are now developing "environmentally friendly" insulation products. I put that in quotes because according to the Department of Agriculture, only 7 percent (*seven!*) of the new bio-based spray foam insulation products needs to come from a renewable resource, such as soybean oil, for it to be labeled "bio-based." That's like saying that only 7 percent of the oats that go into your oatmeal needs to be grown organically for the whole bowl to be labeled "organic." The other 93 percent can be loaded with herbicides and pesticides.

To give it another perspective, if the goal is to conserve the fossil fuels that most of us use to heat our homes, why buy insulation that was produced via the consumption of fossil fuels? Cellulose is a terrific insulation option for existing homes. Straw bale, especially coming from organic crops, makes great sense for new homes and costs very little. There are even ways to wrap an existing house in straw bale for insulation purposes (and to alter its exterior look as well).[11]

Cellulose is a terrific insulation option for existing homes. Straw bale, especially coming from organic crops, makes great sense for new homes and costs very little.

Advantages of Straw Bale as Insulation

A straw bale wall has an R-value (the measure of resistance to the flow of heat) between R-35 and R-45, depending on its thickness. A comparable conventional wall would require ten and a half inches of fiberglass insulation to achieve R-35.

Pricewise, a straw bale wall may be equivalent to a conventional wall since building codes typically require a post-and-beam structure with straw bale as infill only—if they allow them at all. However, consider where the materials come from. Straw bales are made of straw, not to be confused with hay, which is what livestock eat. Straw is what is left in the field after the edible portion of a crop is harvested. The crop doesn't have to be hay either. Wheat, oats, rice—you name it, if it's a grain, it will have straw leftover once it is harvested.

Straw is effectively an agricultural by-product, which gives straw bale building the added benefit of using something that would otherwise go to waste or be burned in the field. I said as much once to a couple of Nebraska farmers who bought me an après-ski drink in a jazz bar just downvalley from the Taos ski resort. They contradicted me and said that straw had plenty of uses, the only of which I remember was bedding livestock. I asked whether there was enough of a straw supply to meet the demand. Too much, they allowed. "What do you do with the rest?" I asked. "Burn it in the field," they answered. I rest my case.

Why not repurpose straw as insulation? If more of us built or retrofitted our homes with straw bale insulation, we would reduce the amount of conventional insulation made from or manufactured or shipped using fossil fuels. Virtually all states have enough agriculture to provide straw bales locally. Mine came from Alamosa, Colorado, an hour up the road from Taos. The cost to buy the bales *and* have them trucked down was less than two thousand dollars. I had some left over after my house was built, which I sold back to Charlie for his next project.

The real point is that it is up to you to carefully consider your options and then choose the best one your conscience will allow. With a little creative thinking, which I sometimes call off-grid thinking, you can reduce your ecological footprint and your heating bill and feel good that you haven't compromised.

Maximizing Your Conservation Potential

For example, applying some creative thinking to the problem of heating your home results in a slew of options for maximizing your conservation potential.

- Live in as small a space as possible. Small spaces require less energy and cost less to heat and cool, not to mention to buy or rent, maintain, insure, and clean. They also help you reduce clutter and make it almost impossible to misplace loose socks, pacifiers, or bank statements.

- Work with Nature, not against her. Choose a house with an east-west axis, which translates to the long walls facing south. Put most of your windows on the south wall, and as few as possible on the north wall. Make sure your roof is south-facing in case you ever want to install solar panels or a living roof (also known as a green roof). Use highly reflective materials for the roof to reduce the heat island effect, a phenomenon where cities are significantly hotter than their surrounding rural areas, in large part because of urban development materials that retain heat. Put a radiant barrier in the attic to discourage heat from the sun from penetrating the house.

Thrifty Green

- Create a tight envelope—i.e., seal all leaks and insulate everything. You can do this yourself if you have time but no money, or hire someone to do it if you have money but no time. Also invest in good-quality windows (which cost money up front but pay dividends multiple times over down the road) and install insulating shades. If you are renting, this is your landlord's job.

- Try to take advantage of passive solar heating. You will need to experiment based on where you live and what your goal is. Are you in a desert climate? Close all windows and insulating shades during the day, then open east and west windows for cross ventilation at night to take advantage of cool air. Open the shades on all south windows if you are trying to heat your house in the winter. Are you in a cold climate? Keep insulating shades on your north windows closed at all times. Keep shades on your south and west windows open, but the windows themselves shut. Put sun-loving plants in your house and see where they thrive. Those are the shades you want open; close the others.

- Ideally use energy from non–fossil fuel sources, whether you or the utility company produces it. If you have the option to select renewable energy sources on your heating bill, do so.

- Make sure all your heating appliances, insulation, windows, and doors meet or preferably exceed code requirements for energy.

- If you have a yard, landscape strategically using deciduous trees for summer shade and winter solar gain. Plant them on the south and west sides.

- Turn the heat down as far as you can stand. Cuddle up with your spouse, child, pet, favorite book, and a clear conscience.

- Heat only the space you use. If you stay in two or three favorite rooms in your house, close the doors and furnace vents to the rooms you never use. If you don't already spend your time in the warmest part of the house, start. If you have cats, they are already there. Or turn your central heat down to fifty degrees and heat your kitchen when you cook, your bathroom with a heated towel rack, and your bed with a down comforter.

- Adjust your idea of how warm you really need to be and put a sweater on.

Remember that you want to work *with* Nature, not against her. The pros include saving energy and money. The cons . . . I can't think of any. A less tangible benefit to passive solar design is that it makes you feel more connected to the earth. If you have to pay attention to opening and closing your windows and shades, then you pay closer attention to sun motion, sun angles, wind patterns, whether the trees have leaves, overnight dips in temperature, hard frosts, midwinter thaws, the return of songbirds, and the first fresh breath of a truly warm wind in the spring. You can't put a price on that.

Where Does Your Heat Come From?

While the best thing you can do is to use less heat to begin with, there is a second half to the equation. It hinges on where your heat comes from. If the energy you use to heat your home is renewable, you can use it with a clear conscience. You are already using less of the earth's non-renewable resources, so keep your house nice and warm.

Monticello: A Passive Solar Home

Passive solar principles are effective in keeping homes cool as well as heating them. Thomas Jefferson put some of the principles to use when designing Monticello, his estate in Virginia. The house had thick masonry walls, windows and doors situated to ensure a good cross breeze, and shaded porches that cooled the air before it entered.

Obviously I am a fan of passive solar heating and cooling. It's clean, renewable, and free. Since the most environmentally friendly thing you can do is not expend energy, and because you don't have to pay for that which you don't consume, free heat from the sun is just about perfect. If you live in a sunny climate, such as large portions of the American West, there is no excuse for not taking advantage of solar gain. Besides, heating your house for free is like finding money in the street.

But what if you live in a cloudy area? Some other heating methods fall in the free and clean category: down comforters, hot beverages, and cuddling up together all have virtually no cost to the environment. If you are frugal, broke, or extremely motivated, all of these may appeal to you. The rest of us are stuck with whatever the utility companies provide, and this depends on the part of the country in which you live.

Whether you consume heating oil, electricity, natural gas, or propane to heat your home, you are using a nonrenewable resource that will eventually run out. Maybe not in this lifetime, but they will. After minimizing your energy consumption for heat, it makes sense to look into different ways to heat your home. Beyond passive solar methods, you have several options, some via your utility company and others do-it-yourself.

As of 2008, utility companies provided only 7.3 percent of our nation's energy, for heat and electricity combined, via renewable resources. Since then, that number has increased and will increase faster with some pressure from energy consumers. However, there are only three ways a utility company can provide renewable heat: geothermal energy, biomass, and with renewable electricity.

Fact:

The word *geyser* comes from the Icelandic *geysir*, the name given to the first known geyser, found in Iceland. *Geysir* is derived from an Icelandic verb meaning "to gush."

Geothermal energy refers to the heat contained within the earth, which breaks through the earth's surface in the form of hot springs, volcanoes, or geysers. There is a swath of geothermal activity in the United States from Yellowstone to the Mexican border. This heat source is as clean and reliable as the sun and is vastly underused in America. It is used very successfully in Iceland, however, a country whose natural resources include hot water and codfish and not much else. Icelanders have tapped their geothermal resources to provide heat and hot water to homes and even to melt snow from roads and sidewalks via radiant tubes underneath their surfaces.[12] Why work against Nature when you can work with her? Why drive a snowplow when you can pipe the hot water that Nature provided under the sidewalk instead?

Geothermal heat is an idea currently being explored in parts of our country where there is potential. If you live in those locales, it would be worth a vote or a letter to your representative to hurry this effort.

Geothermal Energy in Colorado

Aspen, Colorado, has recently proposed to use a geothermal heat pump system in a four-square-mile area of downtown. In addition to using this renewable, carbon-free resource to heat and cool both commercial and residential buildings, the town also proposed to use piped hot water to keep streets and sidewalks clear of snow. This technology will be useful in such a small town during the winter. When you plow snow, you have to pile it somewhere. In banner snow years, the town of Aspen has literally run out of space to put their snow. Melting it is a much better option so it can run into the storm drains right after it hits the ground.

Biomass describes all of the planet's organic matter, including animal waste and trees, plants, algae, and anything else that uses photosynthesis to store the sun's energy within its own matter. Biomass can be used to make "renewable natural gas," another nascent green heating option that is being researched but is not yet commercially viable. As a renewable resource, biomass has the advantage of being able to use the existing natural gas infrastructure, which gives it a leg up on the other options. In the parts of the country that rely on natural gas, renewable natural gas should be an option utility companies are considering. If they aren't, again, it is worth a little pressure from consumers.

Electricity is notorious for being an expensive way to heat a house. Its bad reputation came about in the '70s when electric baseboard heat was popular. I remember laying wool socks out to dry on our baseboards, but that's really all they are good for. Even today, if you are progressive enough to provide your own electricity from a renewable source as I did in Taos, heating your house with it is an inefficient use of it.

In Taos, I could have plugged in a space heater to keep the bathroom warmer, but it would have quickly drained my batteries. I preferred to be able to keep lights on and find a different way to stay warm. I would argue that the tradeoff and solution are the same for a conventional house, unless you install a heat pump. A heat pump is a mechanical device that moves heat from one place to another, refrigerators being the most widely used example. They can operate very efficiently once installed and become an environmental option when powered by renewable electricity, although turning your heat down is still preferable.

Additionally, there are some DIY measures you can take to supplement or replace the heat from the utility company. One option is a woodburning stove like the one I had in Taos, but be careful to check your local regulations because some areas limit the extra pollution produced by woodsmoke. Variations on wood stoves are pellet stoves, ceramic or soapstone stoves, and Russian stoves. These can all be very efficient if you have a small space to heat.[13]

To reduce the amount of heat you use from non-renewable resources, you can (1) insulate your home to keep the heat in, (2) turn down the heat provided by your utility company, which is most likely from nonrenewable sources, and (3) obtain supplemental heat from renewable resources within your reach such as the sun, wood stoves, or cuddling with your pet or a family member. If you simply can't do any of those, you can always (4) put political pressure on your local or state officials to require utility companies to produce more heat from renewable sources. Ultimately, when the nonrenewable sources run out, the utility companies will have to turn to renewable sources anyway.

⟨ 3 ⟩

Power and Light

Should you find yourself in a chronically leaking boat, energy devoted to changing vessels is likely to be more productive than energy devoted to patching leaks.

—Warren Buffett

I HAD LIVED IN TAOS FULL-TIME for only a month when I invited some girlfriends down for a weekend visit to eat good food, shop in Taos's funky boutiques, and just relax. I was looking forward to sharing my house with them (and to gloating a bit about my new low-stress, low-impact lifestyle) and had spent the previous day cleaning and stocking the fridge with goodies. Everything was in place as the sun set a few hours before their arrival, and I took time to unwind quietly on the couch with a good book since I knew the weekend would bring nonstop chatter.

The adobe walls of my little house glowed warmly from the pink-colored incandescent bulbs I had installed in the sconces. The overhead LED fixture was on in the kitchen to brighten up that corner, and the lamp beside the couch gave off a circle of light for me to read by as I sat with my feet up. The small, undercounter bar fridge hummed along with the inverter as it kept our treats chilled. Everything was perfect.

Around nine o'clock I spotted headlights at the far end of my dirt road. They appeared and disappeared as they drew closer, the sagebrush being deceptive in its uniformity. It looks flat but really contains gentle ups and downs and the occasional arroyo through which flash floods channel. I put my book away and stood to monitor their progress. When the approaching car was less than a hundred yards away, my power cut out.

The problem with living in a self-sustaining house is that when the power goes out, you can't just call the power company and complain. If you have a photovoltaic (PV) system with no backup generator, which was my setup, you have to wait until the sun comes up the next day and pray that there are no clouds to impede the charging of your batteries. Also, the sun may rise at 7:00 a.m., but it takes several hours of it striking the solar panels for enough charge to accumulate in the batteries to be useful.

On the other hand, with the exception of the refrigerator, the electric ignition on the propane stove, and the electric pump, I didn't really use electricity during the day. And even those could be mitigated. The electric ignition on the stove was just a convenience: I could light the burners with a match if I needed to. As for the pump, if I conserved water, I could wait a day or so before I needed to refill the pressure tank that served as my indoor water reservoir. It wasn't a problem—the dishes could wait, I could shower at the pool, and double up on toilet flushes or even go outside if I was feeling adventurous.

But the refrigerator was a different story. The night my friends arrived, there was nothing I could do but light some candles, distribute flashlights around the house, and unload the contents of the fridge into a cooler, which I deposited outside the door. Luckily, the nighttime temperature was low enough that the food stayed cold even without ice in the cooler. In fact, it stayed so cold that the orange juice turned into frozen slush.

My friends were gracious about the situation, although one of them had brought her electric breast pump and was forced to sit in the car and use the adapter every time she needed it. She's a good sport, and we had a fun, lively weekend.

But the larger problem of what to do about power consumption loomed after they left. Because my PV setup was designed for weekend use, and because we originally thought I would have a propane refrigerator, I was faced with the reality that the refrigerator, small as it was, used more energy than the system could provide with me living there full-time.

Does this sound familiar? The demand outstripped the supply, only in my case the results were evident immediately. In our planet's collective case, we won't see drastic consequences for a while.

I ran through my options, applying a little off-grid thinking when brainstorming:

1. **Stop eating refrigerated food.**

2. **Store my food in a cooler on the shady north side of the house.**

3. **Use the electric fridge until I ran out of electricity, then stop eating refrigerated food until the batteries recharged.** Repeat every couple of days and live without the other electrical appliances.

4. **Install a full-sized propane fridge in my house.** But where? I only had the nook under the kitchen counter, and there were no propane refrigerators of that size that I could find. There was no convenient place for a larger one. Also, the installation would entail paying not only for the new refrigerator but also to run a propane line halfway around the house outside and cut a vent through my bale wall. Not a pretty picture, and just another place for persistent mice to get in.

5. **Install a propane fridge outside next to the propane tank.** That would be inconvenient, although no more so than the cooler. Also a little weird, even by my standards.

6. **Install more solar panels and batteries and keep using the electric fridge.** This was at least as expensive as the propane refrigerator would be, and it seemed wasteful.

I decided to keep my food in a cooler until fetching it became inconvenient enough to make change imperative. When I lived on-grid before Taos, I would never have considered not eating refrigerated food as an option to save energy. Of course, I was never faced with such a strict conservation scenario where I had to prioritize my power needs.

Thrifty Green

To me, the decision made perfect sense. I didn't have the money to buy either a full-sized propane refrigerator or to upgrade my PV system, which eliminated solutions 4 through 6. Solution 1 wouldn't work because of my addiction to yoghurt and orange juice for breakfast. Solution 3 sounded too dicey since I had other draws on the PV system, and I couldn't chance being out of power for too long since my water supply depended on it. That left solution 2.

I learned a few things about myself after implementing solution 2. First, it was yet another way to keep me in tune with the motion of the sun since I needed to keep the cooler in the shade, especially in the spring and summer. Second, apparently I didn't consider hauling a heavy cooler back and forth to be an inconvenience, even after summer rolled around and I had to move it from one side of the house to the other several times a day. Third, I didn't even find it inconvenient starting in May when I had to buy ice to keep my food cold. Mostly I found it annoying that I was spending money on something like ice. And fourth, I didn't think of myself as eccentric for having to put on a coat, hat, and headlamp to retrieve my dinner in the winter. It made sense and quickly became normal.

Other aspects of life with an intermittent power source became normal as well. I stopped turning on all my lights and learned to use only what I needed. I like to read at night, so the only light I needed was the one lighting the pages of my book. And I didn't even turn that on until the natural light was too dim for me to see properly, which came well after sunset.

One benefit of not using artificial light at dusk was that the animals who crept out of their dens to feed in the sagebrush couldn't see me behind the window glass, and I could watch them unobserved. Cottontail and jack rabbits appeared with regularity, as did the coyotes that hunt them. There was also a covey of nearly twenty quail who came around occasionally, to my delight. On a couple of occasions, they pecked and scratched not three feet from my window bench observation post, oblivious to my presence, and once they settled down for the night under my car. Quail puff up their feathers to stay warm, and it looked like a group of fluffy footballs had congregated haphazardly behind my wheels. Not using light moved me closer to my place in the natural order of things.

Another benefit to keeping my lights off was not contributing to light pollution, a thoughtless, manmade phenomenon with consequences large and small.[14]

Fact:

Light pollution, manmade light that obscures the natural light from the stars and moon, affects wildlife. Sea turtle hatchlings navigate their way to the ocean by the light of the brightest object in the sky: the moon. If manmade lights along the coast compete with it, the hatchlings can become confused and go in the wrong direction instead, getting lost and potentially falling victim to traffic when crossing roads.

If you live in a city, look up at night and find the Orion constellation, the one I find easiest to locate. How many stars does it include? From most locations, you can probably only see seven: three for his belt, with two above and two below representing his limbs. The next time you visit Taos or another location with minimal light pollution, check out Orion again. You will be able to see a sword of multiple stars hanging from his belt, with the whole constellation set against the backdrop of the Milky Way. One of my favorite pastimes in Taos was stargazing, which requires the kind of darkness that doesn't exist in cities. Being able to witness our corner of the universe wheeling overhead on a nightly basis made me feel connected to the whole and that much more alive.

Most of us grid-connected folk are not conscious of how much power we consume. It is simply there for the taking, and in wasting it, we also waste the opportunity to know the undiscovered benefits of conservation.

When the power had cut out and I wanted to read at night, I usually drove into town to an Internet café to share their electricity. I plugged in my cell phone charger, checked my email on the café's computer, and sipped a cup of tea while surrounded by the constant murmur of social chatter. It was a welcome change from the solitude of my house. Other times, though, I preferred to stay at home. So I lit the candles that lived on my breakfast table. It is possible to read by candlelight, if you are motivated enough. You have to hold the book up with the candle in between the pages, then move it back and forth to illuminate the lines you are reading. I only did this a couple of times, but it worked for providing reading light as well as the cooler did for keeping my food cold.

It felt good to be self-sufficient, but I have to admit that whenever I visited friends who were connected to the grid, I envied them their constant supply of electricity. They could flip a switch and lights would come on. They didn't have to think about it. Because I had a limited supply stored in the batteries and no knowledge of how much I had left at any given moment, I had to consciously decide to use power every time I flipped a switch, knowing that I was potentially trading off lights for water replenishment, or using the blender for charging my cell phone.

Life without Power

Olive's shack had no power whatsoever when she first moved in. Her setup was such that she didn't need it. Her refrigerator was propane powered; her light at night came from oil lamps; she used an outhouse and therefore had no electric pump as I did; she charged her phone in her truck; and she otherwise did without. It was not an uncivilized life by any means—just a little outside the norm for this country.

Conscious decision making became a hallmark of my off-grid life. It forced me to slow down, in stark contrast to the previous decade of my life in the hectic corporate world. I stopped multitasking. I didn't absentmindedly turn on all my lights while chatting on my charging cell phone and running the food processor to make dinner. Instead I considered each action singly in terms of energy use. Did I need all the lights on? Could I charge my cell phone the next time I was in my car? Would a knife suffice instead of the food processor? The result was that I gave each action its due and learned to find grace in the humblest of activities. My phone conversations became more meaningful when I paid attention, and my food tasted better when I manually prepared it. It was a pleasant surprise to learn that I reaped rewards far beyond simply conserving my finite supply of electricity.

The earth also has a finite supply of the most abundant nonrenewable resource we use to create electricity: coal. We can estimate how much we have left and how long it will be until we run out, which is several generations from now.

Fact:

According to the Energy Information Administration, America has a 234-year supply of coal at today's rate of consumption. However, the organization calculates an increased rate of consumption of 0.6% per year through 2030. With that growth rate, they recalculate that our reserves will be exhausted in 146 years.[15]

And yet most of us grid-connected folk are not conscious of how much power we consume. It is simply there for the taking, and in wasting it, we also waste the opportunity to know the undiscovered benefits of conservation.

Another fallacy of being connected to the grid is that we assume that those lights will come on every time we flip the switch. We feel entitled to the electricity and complain if there is a brownout or even if rates increase too much. When we don't have to worry about our power supply, we wind up owning all the conveniences and luxuries of modern living: lights, electric appliances (e.g., refrigerators, washers and dryers, dishwashers, water heaters, even baseboard heaters in some cases), TVs, stereos, computers, and any of the myriad gadgets that need to be plugged in to recharge, from cell phones to electric razors. We use them instead of finding other ways to solve our problems—other ways that often end up connecting us more to other people, the planet, and ourselves. And then we keep them all plugged in, drawing a phantom load even when they are not in use. (Any appliance that has a remote control is always "on" at a low level, and therefore draws power called a "phantom load," while being available to receive a signal.)

By contrast, whenever I walked out the door in Taos, my house used no electricity whatsoever. No phantom loads, no lights left on, nothing. Zero impact.

When I moved back on the grid, I made some adjustments in my conservation habits. To be honest, I overcompensated. Electricity is so cheap in this country and so reliable that it is easy to take it for granted. I am now married to a software developer who likes to keep his computer equipment plugged in and on at all times, which I could never have done in Taos with my minimal PV setup. We leave the porch light on at night if we go out, which I also never did in Taos. We own all the standard appliances that I lived without for a year and a couple of extras, like the electric fireplace, along with one that is firmly in the unnecessary luxury category: a wine refrigerator that was a wedding gift.

But there is a difference this time. Now that I have experienced living without the modern conveniences, I don't feel the need to own them and am appreciative when I do. I am also willing to run my life a little outside the American mainstream. For example, we have a tiny kitchen that would be considered normal in Europe but provokes gasps in the United States. It contains a small refrigerator that is shorter than I am and about half as wide as a typical American one. Once you have kept all your food in a cooler, you realize that you can get away with having a fridge not much larger than that, which uses less power than a full-sized one. (What I really like is having a freezer compartment. I could never store ice cream in Taos, especially during the summer. On the other hand, that meant I didn't eat much ice cream, which isn't such a bad thing.)

We also have a dishwasher that looks like it belongs in a doll house. It drives my husband crazy, but since I got used to doing dishes by hand, it's a step up for me. A British friend commented that plenty of European kitchens wouldn't have one at all, so it would be a step up for them as well.

Our washing machine is tucked into a corner of the kitchen, and the dryer is located in the unattached garage—carrying a load of wet wash outside on a snowy day in January to get to the dryer isn't much of a stretch from my Taos experience of stepping outside to fetch breakfast from the cooler. My next project will be to string a clothesline out back and let the sun infuse our clothes with that warm scent you can't get any other way, despite what the makers of dryer sheets advertise.

The wine refrigerator finally got to me. It bothered my husband too. At first we were pleased to own this yuppie luxury item, and we even kept it full of left-over wine from our wedding. The problem was that it cycled on almost constantly. I timed it once: it spent two minutes on for every one minute off. That's when I found my personal threshold of waste. Back on the grid, I turn more lights on than I did in Taos (although I never leave them on in an empty room) and I switch on the electric fireplace for ambience and warmth occasionally. I can plug my phone in to charge without thinking about it, and I don't have the TV on a power strip, although I should so we can power it off completely and eliminate the phantom load when we are not watching it. But I couldn't in good conscience listen to this extraneous appliance suck up power continually, especially when we ran out of wine and put a six-pack of beer in there just to have something in it. Besides, it was noisy. My husband finally unplugged it and moved it to the garage. After we install rooftop solar panels and convert to net metering (see sidebar), we may use it again. In the meantime, we have a refrigerate-as-you-drink policy in our household.

Net Metering

Electricity meters run accurately forward and backward, recording both the consumption and production of electricity. Local regulations vary widely, but it is possible to calculate your "net" usage of electricity (consumption minus production) and pay only for that portion. This is called net metering. If you have solar panels, a small wind turbine, or some other source of energy that can be fed into your power grid connection, it is possible to zero out your power bill by producing more than you consume, if your local laws and consumption habits allow it.

Using Less Power

As with heat, there are three similar ways to use less power that comes from nonrenewable resources:

1. **Alter your consumption habits.**

2. **Produce your own electricity from renewable sources.**

3. **Lobby your local or state government to require a higher percentage of power produced by public utilities to come from renewable sources.**

Fact:

According to the U.S. Department of Energy, houses consume 20 percent of the energy in the United States.

The first option is the most accessible to everybody because it involves simple behavior changes and no financial investment. Take light bulbs, the most familiar and obvious example. People like to debate the quality of light provided by compact fluorescent light bulbs versus incandescent ones. But why turn the lights on at all, especially during the day? What about the quality of natural light?

It has more variety and more subtlety than anything humans can produce. Starlight is dim; moonlight is cold. Sunlight . . . depends. On a late autumn afternoon, it is warm and mellow, the best sort of light for flattering

The Hype Surrounding Compact Fluorescent Light Bulbs

It's the first thing that occurs to us when we think of conserving energy in the home: switch from incandescent to compact fluorescent bulbs. While compact fluorescents use significantly less electricity than incandescent bulbs emitting a similar amount of light, that's not the end of the story. I am referring neither to their price, nor to their reliability or disposal issues. CFLs are only more efficient because they put out more light and less heat for each watt of electrical energy that goes into them. Is that good? It depends on how you look at it. As anyone who has ever made brownies with an Easy-Bake Oven knows, incandescents put out quite a bit of heat. During the winter, if you live in a cold climate, the heat generated by your incandescents is offset by less heat having to be provided by your furnace. If you switch to CFLs, you may use less energy for light but more to run your furnace more often. Calculating how much energy you have saved is a topic for hairsplitters. So don't be too quick to pat yourself on the back for helping to save the environment. This sort of "conservation" is largely cosmetic. For true energy savings, turn your lights off.

pictures. At high noon on a summer's day, it can be harsh and glaring. At midday in winter, depending on your location and latitude, it glances off snowdrifts and scatters like shards of glass. At sunrise it is fresh; at sunset, there are as many types of light produced as there are stale ways to describe them. Low light at dusk obscures; at dawn, it illuminates.

When you keep your lights off, you notice these subtle differences. You also quickly figure out where the sun penetrates your house, which is where you want to sit to work and stay warm. Using less power for lights (or none at all) is the easiest, cheapest way to conserve.

The same idea applies to appliances. It would be interesting to try a little off-grid thinking here. Imagine that you are required to produce all the electricity that you use. What would you do differently on the consumption side? Personally, I would unplug every single appliance in my house or put them on a power strip that could be shut off when they weren't in use. All of them. Including the refrigerator occasionally just for fun. When I did use them, it would be as infrequently as possible and only when I couldn't come up with a creative alternative solution.

The energy you don't use is the cheapest, and conservation-minded behavior changes cost nothing. Too often, egged on by advertisers and our consumer culture, we seek to buy a fancy gadget to do the conserving for us. But don't be too wowed by high-tech solutions if you are looking to go green and save money. If you are willing to make some conscious decisions, you can do most of it yourself for free.

> *The energy you don't use is the cheapest, and conservation-minded behavior changes cost nothing.*

For example, a "smart" refrigerator—one that connects to public utilities and runs more efficiently during peak demand hours—makes ice only during off-peak hours, saving energy and money. Why not own a small, cheap, "dumb" refrigerator that doesn't have an icemaker? You can fill ice trays at any hour you choose and save both the initial investment and the life cycle cost (at least where icemakers are concerned) of the "smart" refrigerator.

"Smart" dishwashers similarly will delay running until off-peak hours unless overridden by the human involved. But peak power hours are typically from 3 p.m. to 8 p.m. Why not run your dishwasher right before you go to bed or first thing in the morning? And only then if it's full. Or get rid of it and do your dishes by hand.

Supposedly these "smart" appliances, also known as "demand-response" appliances, benefit the power grid by leveling the demand on it, which obviates the need for power plants that operate only during extreme demand times and lessens the chance of power outages. But smart power consumers can have the same effect by reducing their demand without spending a dime on new appliances. Note too that the goal should be to *reduce* power consumption, not level it out over time. The very idea of leveling demand assumes that America's population will continue our status quo of wasteful power consumption. Why not use less?

There is always an option to solve your problem through conservation and without spending money (or spending as much money as a high-tech appliance costs). Doing laundry is another example. Before you even get to the point where you need to do a load of laundry, you can make sure you have worn your clothes more than once, taking care to keep them as clean as possible. In my experience, clothes worn to an office can stand to be worn multiple times if you don't sweat in them or spill

Doing Dishes by Hand

Depending on how you do it, washing dishes by hand can be either efficient or inefficient. And depending on how you look at it, it can be either a chore or an opportunity for meditation. In Taos, I had to do my dishes by hand. The method I employed for doing them conserved both energy and water.

First, I boiled a kettle of water on the propane stove. While it was heating, I filled a dish tub with one inch of cold water from the tap and added soap to make it sudsy. I topped that off with boiling water to a depth of two inches. The stack of dirty dishes on the counter went into the suds one by one, with the occasional addition of water from the kettle to keep it hot, before being restacked in a separate pile.

When they had all been cleaned with hot soapy water, I turned the tap on so a thin stream of cold water came out—not full blast, never full blast. I rinsed the dishes under this trickle, paying careful attention to wipe the soap off, and then placed them in the dish drainer to air-dry.

Lastly, I poured the remaining sudsy water into the sink, scrubbing it along with the dishpan, and rinsed it all down with what was left in the kettle.

Total energy expended: two minutes' worth of propane burning to boil the water, plus fifteen minutes' worth of elbow grease to do the dishes.

on them. The clothes you put on when you come home from work for a handful of hours before you go to bed can stand multiple wearings too. Unless you are working out in them or staining them in some way, your clothes don't need to be washed every time you wear them.

Then, when it does come time to wash them, make sure you have a full load. If you find yourself doing a small load of laundry because you want to wear your lucky t-shirt to poker night, wash it alone by hand instead. All it takes is a little conscious thought.

When I lived in Taos, where I had no washer and dryer, hauling my laundry to the Laundromat was enough of a chore that I did laundry about once a month, if that. The limiting factor was underwear, which I easily washed by hand and hung up to dry whenever I was on the verge of running out. I don't actually own that many clothes; I just keep them clean and wash them sparingly, which, incidentally, prolongs their life.

The point of this digression is that I paid neither for these appliances nor for the power to run them. I shared the latter expense with the customers of the local Laundromat, and then as little as possible. Even on-grid in suburbia, this is a solution.

Sources of Power

I have a confession to make. My house in Taos is now connected to the grid. Toward the end of my year off the grid, my batteries died and I ran out of power. I could have simply replaced them, but the need to tinker with my PV system led me to consider upgrading the whole thing, including the electric refrigerator, to support full-time living, assuming I could find the money. The reality is that if you are anywhere close to the grid, it will provide your cheapest source of power. Olive discovered that when she finally decided she wanted electric lights in her shack, around the same time my system was dying. But whenever she mentioned a PV system to her electrician friend, he always asked her about connecting to the grid instead, an idea that galled her.

Olive, like me, doesn't like to be dependent on anyone, including utility companies. Also like me, she enjoyed not having any utility bills. But mostly she had trouble squaring her conscience with the dirty energy provided by the power company. (New Mexico gets the bulk of its power from coal. To find out where your state's power comes from, check out the map on National Public Radio's website. [16]) But it was her cheapest option once she gave in to the convenience of having electricity. In the intervening years between when I bought my land and when Olive wanted power, Joaquin had paid to bring the grid almost to my lot line so he could build some more houses. (My solitary paradise had begun to disappear.) Olive found out, to her dismay, that stringing it the rest of the way was cheaper than installing a complete PV system.

Olive had another problem as well: she wanted to sell a couple acres of her land. Not many people are interested in buying land with no power or water source, and bringing the grid to her lot line would make it more salable. If she was going to do that, she reasoned, she might as well string it all the way out to the shack. Once she had made that decision, she needed my approval to dig a trench and lay cable across my land. I gave it to her and then decided that I would connect too since I needed to do something about my lack of power. It solved my refrigerator problem, albeit in a way I had not envisioned.

I really like the idea of supplying all my own power, or even producing more than I consume as a way to give back to my country. This is cheapest and easiest to do if I have already reduced my consumption. In Taos or Colorado, where I live now, the climate is suited to PV systems. The sun is out a lot, which is convenient but by no means a requirement. Even if your skies are largely cloudy, if you reduce your electricity consumption enough, installing solar panels may cover or at least offset your power needs, especially if you consider your total power consumption and production over the course of a year.

But there are other options depending on where you live and what your circumstances are. For example, if you have a nearby stream on your property, you can install a microhydro system, essentially a small-scale hydroelectric plant that can power a house or set of houses.

Valley View Hot Springs, Colorado

At Valley View Hot Springs, now the Orient Land Trust, all of the electricity at the resort is provided by an on-site hydroelectric plant. *Resort* may be overstating it, though. The hot springs are privately owned and were first developed in the '70s as a "naturist" retreat—meaning clothing optional (which means nude). Not just in the hot springs, but everywhere on the grounds. The people who frequent Valley View like it that way.

They also like the minimal ecological footprint achieved right from the beginning. The owners first installed a small waterwheel thirty years ago to power a few lights and play some music. By the '80s, the electrical demand had grown, and a larger hydro plant was built. The water from the hot springs flows down a steep hillside with enough force to be channeled into hydroelectric turbines. Twenty years later, it has been updated and expanded twice to keep up with increased demand.

Valley View uses no fossil fuels except in a few of their larger vehicles. The environmental practices established here during the '70s, the time of our last energy crisis, have served the property well.

If you have a windy location and the conditions are right, you can do home wind power with a small turbine. We actually considered this when batting around different designs for my house in Taos since the mesa where the house is located has strong, consistent winds. We decided against it because wind turbines are noisy and they have moving parts, which can break. Solar panels are quiet and have no moving parts.

Another idea for wind power is to join together with other members of your community and create a wind turbine cooperative. In a traditional wind farm, the owner of the development leases land from community members or pays them royalties but retains all other rights and profits. In a wind turbine cooperative, the project is jointly owned by the landowners who share in the decisions and the profits.

However, I predict that most people will not have the means to supply their own power. Therefore, the onus will ultimately fall on the public utilities to convert to power produced by renewable resources. These could include solar panel arrays, such as those installed in various parts of the American West; wind farms, including offshore wind farms like those being proposed in Massachusetts; hydroelectricity from existing dams such as those in the Pacific Northwest; or even geothermal electricity generated in Iceland, for example.

Our nation is large and its resources varied. The solution for renewable power will likewise vary from one area of the country to another. The real point is that the solution is well within our grasp if we get started on it now.

As citizens, we can put pressure on lawmakers to require the production of power from renewable resources such as those listed above. Getting the technology and infrastructure to a useful point will require an investment

The Blue Lagoon

Iceland is not known for its abundance of natural resources. However, its hot springs, geysers, and (now famously) volcanoes are all evidence of a natural resource that will be increasingly valuable in the future: geothermal energy. Just outside of Reykjavik is the granddaddy of all hot springs: the Blue Lagoon, so named for the color that results from the blue-green algae reflecting off the white silica mud on the bottom.

To generate electricity, steam is recovered from the water of this and other hot springs and piped through steam turbines. As an electricity source, it is both reliable and clean, producing no greenhouse gases.

in universities, public utilities, and private companies to give them the funding and impetus they need, especially to overcome the tendency to perpetuate the status quo. Fossil fuel supplies are finite, no matter how creatively we access and consume them. They will run out. So investing our time, money, and energy in innovation with them simply pushes the problem into the future, and that's not a very nice thing to do to your grandchildren. (As the Arab saying goes, "My father rode a camel. I drive in a limousine. My son flies a jet. His son will ride a camel.") Extracting oil from tar sands in Canada, for example, and developing "clean" coal technology merely prolong the inevitable and come with their own environmental costs. It's analogous to transferring your credit card balance from one card to the next for as long as your credit holds out. At some point you have to pay your debt.

Our global debt is mounting and will continue to increase along with the world's population. We need to find a sustainable solution, and quickly. The pace of research is unpredictable, even with funding. Maybe the solution is right around the corner.

A Role for Nuclear Power?

Steven Chu, the U.S. secretary of energy, wrote an opinion piece in the *Wall Street Journal* (March 23, 2010) in which he advocated for "small modular reactors" (SMRs). These are essentially compact, transportable nuclear reactors that could be used to supplement or replace existing fossil fuel power plants. Built in factories and shipped to the designated locations, SMRs are designed to be cleaner, safer, more reliable, and more efficient than older nuclear technology. I mention them here in the interest of putting all options on the table.

American opinion remains tainted by the Three Mile Island debacle in 1979 and the specter of the Chernobyl meltdown in 1986. People object to the waste (there is waste involved in coal extraction and burning—remember acid rain?) and to health and safety risks for nuclear plant workers (How many people have died in coal mine accidents in the past ten years alone? How many suffer from lung disease?). The biggest fear is that of a radiation leak that contaminates surrounding areas and the people who live there. Yet France currently gets nearly 80 percent of its electricity from its fifty-nine nuclear plants, which it also exports to other countries in Europe, and its contamination record is as good as other energy sources (BP oil spill in the Gulf of Mexico, anyone?). Nuclear power is not perfect, but neither is any manmade solution.

Maybe we go with grid-connected solar, which Joaquin tells me is the wave of the future in his native Germany. Or maybe it's a hodgepodge of renewable energy sources that depends on what is available regionally. Or maybe it's something we haven't come up with yet. But I know one thing: in the meantime, the best thing we can do is use less.

🖙 **4** 🖎

Water

When the well's dry, we know the worth of water.

—Benjamin Franklin

WHEN I REACHED THE END of my year off the grid, not only had I run out of power, I had also run out of water. The two are inextricably linked at my house because of the electric pump. Jason, who was to become my husband when I moved back on the grid, came down for a visit from Colorado one weekend in late fall of 2007. Ironically, there was plenty of water in the cistern since I had not had enough electricity to run the pump much at all for the previous couple of months. I just couldn't get it into the house short of lowering a bucket into the cistern, which was going to be my last resort. By the time Jason arrived, even the pressure tank—my indoor reservoir—was completely empty.

I had renewed admiration for Olive, who lived with no running water at the shack. While my catchment setup necessitated conservation, at least I had running water, which I had apparently been taking for granted even in the small amounts I was using it. I had stopped watering my garden, and I never showered at home. I had even taken to going to the bathroom outside during the day. (The sagebrush is vast and empty. The only observers were rabbits and coyotes, and they were far more interested in each other.) In a fitting reversal of the general order, Olive offered to let me use her outhouse.

She also took pity on me and lent me a five-gallon plastic jug, the kind she used to haul all of her water. I was too cheap to buy my own since I knew power (and therefore water) was coming once the utility company finished pulling the line out to the shack. In the meantime, I slashed my water consumption to the minimum possible and purchased water at the grocery store at thirty-nine cents per gallon. They had a dispenser of purified water from which I would refill Olive's jug and carry it home.

Water is heavy. At roughly eight pounds per gallon, the jug weighed over forty pounds. It took all my effort to heave it onto the kitchen counter, where I poured it into smaller, more manageable pitchers. One resided in the bathroom for use when brushing my teeth. Another stayed in the kitchen for washing dishes. When Jason arrived, I let him do the carrying and heaving.

Jason has an easygoing attitude. Without complaint, he went without a shower the entire weekend and used the great outdoor toilet as much as possible.

But sometimes—use your imagination here—you really want to use an indoor, sit-down toilet, after which you need to flush it. Since initially the toilet bowl and tank contained water, it flushed with no problem the first time. The second time, it didn't refill like it needs to for the next use. We had to pour water in the tank for that to happen.

Seventeen Days without a Shower

When I went to Nepal, I spent seventeen days high in the mountains, walking narrow footpaths and staying at teahouses with no running water. The first few nights after we reached our destination, a porter would bring a bowl of hot washing water to the weary trekkers so we could freshen up and pretend we were staying clean. After a day or two, it turned into cold washing water. Then it disappeared entirely.

When I asked my guide about it, he informed me that hot water was a luxury in mountain villages. Teahouses would burn wood for fires to heat water—just a waste of a scarce resource—so Western trekkers could bathe. Some teahouses even had "showers" that involved a tank of freshly heated water and gravity to produce the stream of water we were used to. My trekking companion tried it and found it to be an unsatisfactory trickle, not worth the expense of natural resources and energy.

I simply went without showering. After a week, I could smell my own body odor. Shortly after that, I got used to it and no longer noticed it. But the most surprising discovery came when we trekked back to Lukla, the village with a runway where most trekkers begin and end their Everest-region journeys. As we headed into town, we passed a group of trekkers fresh off the plane. I knew they had just started because they distinctly smelled of soap, shampoo, conditioner, deodorant, laundry detergent, and all the other artificial aromas that perfume Westerners and cover their natural scent. It had never before occurred to me that the products we use to make ourselves smell "clean" may in fact make us smell funny to people who don't use them.

So Jason filled a pitcher with water from the plastic jug, and we poured it into the tank, where it made no appreciable difference. We poured in another one. Then another, and another. By the time we filled the tank, we had drained the plastic jug by three gallons. Sixty percent of our water had literally gone down the toilet in the most direct relationship between water and money that I have ever witnessed. I was equal parts alarmed and horrified.

At thirty-nine cents per gallon, this was the most expensive water I had ever paid for. Check your water bill and see what you pay. Now boost the cost to thirty-nine cents per gallon, recalculate the total, and ask yourself how much less you would use if it cost that much.[17] Currently in the Denver area, connected to a city water system, we pay roughly two-tenths of a cent per gallon (plus fixed charges such as storm-water drainage and administrative costs). On the bill I checked to make these calculations, we used approximately 750 gallons for the month. At thirty-nine cents per gallon, that water would have cost almost three hundred dollars, compared to the actual fifty-three-dollar bill. That was some unbelievably expensive water.

Don't kid yourself: when it becomes scarce, it will cost that much. The cost of water supplied by a municipality includes the water supply itself (including water rights), electrical power to run wells and pumps, water treatment costs (such as chemicals), soft costs (such as engineering, legal fees, salaries, insurance), infrastructure (wells, storage tanks, reservoirs, waste plants, pipelines, pumps), and storm-water control. Notice that what you pay for water reflects plans for securing more water in the future in anticipation of a shortage. Don't kid yourself about that either: when you couple unrestrained consumption with increased population growth, water will become scarce.

Securing Water for the Future

The problem of securing water for the future is a tricky one, especially in a state like Colorado that has intricate and arcane water rights and laws. To illustrate, the Donala Water and Sanitation District supplies water to a tiny enclave just north of Colorado Springs. They are in the enviable position of servicing an area of land that is "built-out," meaning that it won't see a population increase in the future. That makes for easier planning. Easier, but by no means easy. Their water supply is currently dependent on the Denver Basin deep water aquifers, which are a depleting resource. Other water districts take water from the Denver Basin as well, which leaves the Donala District vulnerable to increases in its depletion beyond their control. To plan for the future, even though their water supply is holding steady for now, Donala is looking at several solutions, including:

- Purchasing a ranch in the Colorado mountains several hundred miles away for its claim on snowmelt that feeds into the Arkansas River and can be delivered (at an additional expense) to their users

- Joining a consortium of irrigation ditch companies along the same river and securing a junior water right demand on that water

- Pumping water back from the Colorado River (which would also carry a delivery infrastructure cost, as well as water rights costs)

- Treating their own wastewater for potable uses

Our Most Overlooked Natural Resource

When we think of what we need to sustain our current way of life, water is the natural resource we most overlook. As I confirmed living off the grid, we can function without heat, and we can live without power, but we can't survive without water.

It may be several generations from now that we actually feel the pinch from a scarcity of oil and other fossil fuels, but water shortages are here already. Droughts punctuate the seasons of the western states, and even Atlanta, Georgia, in the humid South has an issue with water shortage. These are thorny problems with complex solutions, due in part to antiquated water rights laws.

In my case, I simply needed to wait until the power line was in. What I overlooked, however, was the fact that once it ran down my lot line on its way to the shack, I still needed to get it from the electrical box over to my house, and that required hiring a contractor who knew his way around connecting PV systems to the grid. Fortunately, they abound in Taos. I made an appointment and resigned myself to carrying water five gallons at a time for another couple of weeks. (Taos moves on its own version of "island time.")

In the meantime, Olive came to my rescue again. She was faced with the same hookup issue, but she was out of money, so she simply ran an extension cord from the outlet on the electrical box to her house. I hadn't noticed it until she pointed it out. Problem solved! I had to go to the hardware store to buy a heavy-duty, outdoor cord that I dragged from the electrical box over fifty feet of sagebrush, through a window, and across the width of my house to the bathroom closet. The loveliest sound in the world was my pump finally running again after months with no water. Within five minutes I had flushed the

> *If some of us conserve but others*
> *continue to waste water, it will still*
> *run dry. As the saying goes, if you*
> *are not part of the solution, you*
> *are part of the problem. It is espe-*
> *cially true where water supplies are*
> *concerned.*

toilet and hopped in the shower. And I had vowed never to take running water for granted again.

Even before I had to buy water, I still made an effort to conserve because I could walk out back and look at my finite water supply. In Taos, I always faced the threat of running out of water. In a sense, my house there mirrors the plight of the American West. Or of the earth, if you think about it.

Think beyond the borders of your backyard for a minute. Expand your idea of a neighborhood to include your home state, our entire country, the continent it resides on, and the planet itself. This neighborhood has a finite amount of water for all its residents to share. It is a closed-loop system: after I use some water, I send it downstream to you. Surface water evaporates and rises to the sky, where it eventually recondenses and falls back to earth. Some of it pools in lakes and rivers, or blankets the tops of mountains with snow, and some recharges underground aquifers. But it's all connected. And the more demand we place on the system, the sooner it will run dry.

If some of us conserve but others continue to waste water, it will still run dry. As the saying goes, if you are not part of the solution, you are part of the problem. It is especially true where water supplies are concerned.

Because of the possibility of running out in Taos, I not only made sure I conserved water, but I also kept track of rain, snowfall, and extended dry periods. Over the course of four seasons, I tuned my senses to the rhythm of my surroundings and adjusted my behavior when necessary.

We all have the opportunity to do the same, even on the grid. Step outside and take a good look at what your surroundings provide. Examine your actions through the lens of Nature and ask yourself if you really want to perpetuate the status quo or whether you could find a way to reduce your water consumption.

In Taos, the water for all of my household uses, including drinking, came from the sky in the form of rain or snow. While my biggest concern was quantity, I also wondered about its quality. I reasoned that it was fine for bathing, brushing teeth, and doing dishes because it was filtered and because the source seemed reasonably pure. Short of acid rain, which doesn't plague New Mexico as far as I am aware, there doesn't seem to be a lot that could pollute or contaminate water that falls from the sky.

But for drinking, I wasn't so bold. There are dedicated drinking water taps on the bathroom and kitchen sinks, and water flowing to them passes through a second filter in addition to the one that filters all incoming water. Despite the double filters, I didn't trust the water enough to drink it. Instead I bought a water dispenser with a ceramic base and a glass bottle that I refilled at the grocery store. It held three gallons, which was all I could hoist onto my shoulder when I replaced the bottle after having refilled it. (Glass is a lot heavier than plastic.)

Playing the Odds

I will take the occasional calculated risk. This is certainly true for my failure to get health insurance when I lived off the grid, but also in small ways when I'm trying to prove a point, even to myself. Take a water-borne parasite called giardia, for example. It is found in alpine streams and lakes and causes gastro-intestinal distress if ingested. Hikers and backpackers are advised to carry their own water or to filter or purify water from a natural source before drinking it. The way I figure it, because giardia originates in animal manure, to enter the water supply the animals have to defecate in or near the mountain streams. Even if they have, it's not guaranteed that you will acquire giardia by drinking that water because the parasites may not actually be present in the sample that you drink. Mountain streams are fast moving and continually replenished by snowmelt. I once tested my theory that the risk was small by drinking from a stream of snowmelt on a spring day at Taos Ski Valley. It was fresh and clean, as pure as water gets. I didn't come down with giardiasis.

But that was an experiment I did once by choice. When it comes to community water supplies, I don't want to play the odds. I want my water to be free from contaminants.

It also tasted fresh and pure, unlike any water I have tasted outside of a mountain stream of snowmelt. When was the last time you commented on the sweet taste of a cool glass of water? The water that flows out of your tap is potable—theoretically—but does it taste good?

Do you know where your drinking water comes from and how it is treated to make it safe to drink? Depending on the source, drinking water in the United States, before treatment, may be subject to industrial pollution (i.e., chemicals), agricultural runoff (i.e., fertilizer, herbicides, pesticides, and organic waste), sewage (treated or untreated), and storm-water runoff (the water you see flowing down street gutters and into storm drains). Untreated water, again depending on the source, may also contain natural contaminants such as bacteria, viruses, algae, salt, and trace minerals, of which the most commonly known is fluoride.[18]

After treatment, the amount of these contaminants is limited by government standards for health and "aesthetic" qualities such as appearance, odor, and taste. But I have encountered cloudy water, sulfur-smelling water, and water with a metallic taste all from municipal water flowing from residential taps. In Taos, my water sometimes smelled a little musty, and I worried that rain and snowmelt washed old bird droppings off the roof and into my cistern. Hence my decision to drink water purified by reverse osmosis that I bought at the store.

Olive also bought water at the natural food store. But since she had to buy it for all her needs, not just drinking, she carried hers in five-gallon plastic jugs. (They don't make glass jugs that big; they would be too heavy to lift.) One day she took a drink from my water dispenser and exclaimed how different—and much better—it tasted than hers. The difference between storing water in glass and ceramic, both inert substances, versus plastic, which leaches taste and who knows what else, was obvious.

Conserving water to me is now second nature. Because it's mostly a matter of habit, once those habits

Water Quality

Worrying about the quantity of water is not enough. Quality matters as well. Here in America we have regulations that, in theory, protect our water quality so we can drink it or put it to other use without fear of contamination that will make us sick or pollution that will harm our bodies or environment. I say "in theory" because pollution in America's water is on the rise. The *New York Times* recently published a series of articles that focused on this topic.[19] Some of the scary article titles include "Rulings Restrict Clean Water Act, Hampering E.P.A."; "Tap Water Can Be Unhealthy but Still Legal"; "Millions in U.S. Drink Contaminated Water, Records Show"; "Sewers at Capacity, Waste Poisons Waterways"; "Cleansing the Air at the Expense of Waterways"; "Health Ills Abound as Farm Runoff Fouls Wells"; "Pollution Grows with Little Fear of Punishment"; and "Debating How Much Weed Killer Is Safe in Your Water Glass." I thought these were topics that applied only in Third World countries whose governments didn't take care of their citizens' most basic needs. Didn't we in the United States open our eyes in 1962 when Rachel Carson published *Silent Spring* (a book I read while living off the grid)? Why are we not guaranteed clean, fresh, healthy water to drink?

are ingrained, they are easy to keep and hard to break. These days, back on the grid, I still shower every couple of days and flush every other time. I cannot be induced ever to run the kitchen tap at full blast, and it pains me to watch someone else do so unnecessarily.

Options for Purer Water

If you are concerned about the quality of your water, what are your options? Of course you could buy bottled water, but this is a huge waste of nonrenewable resources (i.e., petroleum products) if you buy water in plastic bottles. Sure, you can recycle the bottles, but why generate the waste to begin with? Here are some more environmentally friendly options:

- Put a filter on your tap.[20]

- Do water catchment and filter/purify what you catch. Research whether this is safe in your region and whether there are regulations on water catchment.

- Buy a refillable water dispenser, preferably made from ceramic and glass, and fill it with filtered, purified water from a reliable source.

- Pressure your government representatives at the federal, state, and local levels to tighten water quality standards, regulation, and enforcement. This issue is one of the most basic health imperatives.

It similarly pains me here in the arid West to see a lush green lawn like most people still have, even if there is a discreet sign out front letting the rest of us know they are using well water. So what? Ultimately, it's all connected.

My husband and I deliberately bought a house with only two pocket handkerchief–sized lawn areas out front, and no sprinkler system. One of the pocket handkerchiefs, in fact, gets so much hot afternoon sunlight in the summer that it is brittle and dry by July. It would require more water to keep it alive than it is worth. Our plan is to replace it with a flagstone sitting area with a birdbath, a sundial, and some container plants. The rest of the front yard is xeriscaped.

Ingrid and Frank

I have friends in Colorado Springs, Ingrid and Frank, whose personal sensibilities seamlessly united when they got married. Ingrid teaches elementary school and Frank sells used cars. They met because they are both competitive athletes—she in triathlons and he in cyclocross. Their respective sports dominate their lives and discretionary money, and neither one has the desire to spend extravagantly on anything else. Besides, Ingrid comes from frugal German stock and has a hard time paying full price for something she can get on sale. Frank simply isn't materialistic, except where bike gear is concerned. Frank is also interested in being kind to the environment, especially if that goal coincides with his hobby. He likes to bike to work so he can sell cars to other people.

Now, with two children and a suburban house next to a park, Ingrid and Frank are making decisions that combine both of their goals. When Ingrid needed a new car, they bought a Prius. It saved gas (for Frank) and therefore money (for Ingrid). Frank took a class on xeriscaping from their public utility so he could landscape the front yard to save water and money (including water bill reduction plus a tax rebate) and avoid the hassle of maintaining a lawn.[21]

Any future decisions Ingrid and Frank make involving using and paying for the earth's resources will likely combine their twin conservation goals.

Xeriscaping should not be confused with "zero-scaping" either in pronunciation or in definition. When people hear the word *xeriscape*, they sometimes hear a *zero* on the front, as in zero plants in the yard and zero curb appeal for the house. But xeriscaping does not involve a yard full of gravel and cactus. It refers to landscaping with plants that require no supplemental water beyond what Nature provides in order to thrive. Usually these are plants indigenous to the area, but they don't have to be.[22]

In our case, it means a small slope of low-water-use groundcovers with varying textures and colors. Some of them produce flowers and others fruit, such as strawberries. Distributed among the groundcovers are xeric perennials such as blue flax, catmint, salvia, and basket-of-gold. We even have a few iris that pop up in the spring and one errant tulip that managed to establish itself with no help from us. A large locust tree shades half the garden in the summer. The effect is that of an eye-pleasing meadow.[23]

Personally, xeriscaping appeals to me because it means I can have a lovely garden that requires little effort on my part and no extra water (i.e., money). Lazy and cheap—that's me. It's also a way to claim conservation kudos without trying very hard.

Fact:

One hour of watering a lawn uses 220 gallons of water. At thirty-nine cents per gallon (the price I paid for water in Taos when I had to purchase and carry it home from the store, and a good estimate for the price we'll have to pay when inevitably municipal water is scarce), that's $85.80.

I recently read that Denver-area residents waste more than half their water on lawns, and I suspect that is the case for the rest of the country as well.[24] Now there's an easy conservation fix: get rid of your lawn. Replace it with xeric plants that attract butterflies, hummingbirds, and songbirds; watch your water bill go down and your contact with Nature go up. Just spending time in a garden with your feet up and a cool drink in your hand qualifies as free psychotherapy. If you have planted or tended the garden yourself, you can add a sense of pride and satisfaction to the list of intangible benefits.

There's a saying from the Old West, "Whisky's for drinkin'; water's for fightin'." The biggest battles of the future will be fought over water, not oil. Here in Colorado, our three main rivers east of the Rockies where the big cities—Fort Collins, Denver, Colorado Springs, and Pueblo—lie are "overappropriated." Bluntly stated, this means the demand for water by these urban areas often exceeds the available supply. Today. Not at some point in the future. Reservoirs exist, which serve the same function as my cistern in Taos, but keeping them full is a problem. Also like my cistern, if the reservoirs are drained faster than they are refilled, they will dry up. It's an obvious problem with an obvious solution (i.e., collectively use less water), but no one seems to be taking it seriously.

The biggest battles of the future will be fought over water, not oil.

Colorado recently pulled out of a seven-year-long drought. We were three years into it before the authorities imposed water-use restriction. Forward-thinking politicians with backbones (a dying breed) would have made those restrictions permanent, but that didn't happen. Now it's business (or consumption) as usual, and we risk having a serious water shortage in the near future. Saving water in our reservoirs is like saving money in the bank, but how many people do you know who diligently set aside 10 percent of each paycheck to cover a future shortfall?

The same population that won't save money also won't save water if it is left up to them and their good intentions, especially because an under-the-radar problem with no identifiable bad guy never makes headlines. (Identifying yourself as the bad guy is difficult to swallow.)

Occasionally an article will appear with some troubling news buried several pages deep. For example, according to Denver's *Westword* newspaper, "recently, experts discovered that the aquifers have been dropping at an alarming rate" and thus cannot provide the hundred years' supply of water that we originally thought they would.[25] The assistant director for water at Colorado's Department of Natural Resources calls it a "crisis."

A different source, Colorado's Statewide Water Supply Initiative (SWSI), predicts that by 2030, demand for water will exceed supply by almost 20 percent.[26] But the general public never reads the SWSI reports.

Fact:

In the October 2009 issue of *Consumer Report*, it's reported that "almost four in five states anticipate water shortages by 2013."

Thrifty Green

Colorado is not the only state in this boat. One weekend in Taos, when I was limping along on limited power and could run my pump only once a day because of it, I hosted my mother and two of her friends for a weekend visit. I barely had been making ends meet in terms of water before they arrived, and it hadn't really felt like a sacrifice. Once my house's population increased, however, the demand was too great, and the pump couldn't keep up. We had to conserve in the usual ways (no showers, flushing every other time, doing dishes using one kettle of water heated on the stove), but I sweated the entire weekend because I knew our water supply was insufficient. This is the case globally too as populations increase and water supplies become increasingly overtaxed.

The solution is to use less. But in addition to conserving water at home (and at the office, school, day care, church, and everywhere you go), it would be prudent to educate yourself on water issues in your state or local water district. Water use is governed by law and sometimes by agreements between local or regional water boards.[27] They are slow to act, and even when they do make a decision, infrastructure changes are slow to be put in place, not to mention expensive. In fact, your local authorities (if they are farsighted) are probably already putting the wheels in motion for future water regulation in your area right now. If you don't want to be caught with your swim trunks down, now is the time to voice your opinions on water use, conservation, and regulation. If you wait until new laws are enacted—effectively until someone else tells you how to conserve—it will be too late.

If you do look into your local water issues, you may find some startling facts. For example, according to the December 2009 issue of *5280* magazine, when some of

Colorado's arcane, convoluted water laws were drafted, such as those in the 1922 Colorado River Compact, it was predicted that the Colorado River would have 16.4 million water acres per year coursing through the state. More recent predictions adjusted this figure to 12.7 million water acres annually. Whether the first number was simply inaccurate or the second is due to climate change is moot. We now have vastly more people placing much higher demands on a smaller water supply than anticipated. I guarantee this is happening outside of Colorado as well.

Again, think of three extra houseguests placing demands on the finite amount of water in my cistern. As an analogy, it's as if you made $1,640 per month as a single person, then got married and had two kids, only to watch your salary be reduced to $1,270 per month. What would you do? Personally, I would start watching my pennies. In Colorado's case, that means using less water.

It may sound all doom and gloom, but here's a more heartening fact: according to the SWSI report, if Coloradoans all practiced conservation right now, we could close the projected supply-demand gap without having to build any new reservoirs. In other words, without having to spend any money, disturb the earth, or use any more of the planet's resources or energy. What a great idea.

Ways to Conserve Water

There are many ways to practice water conservation beyond replacing your lawn. Once I moved back on the grid and had access to a larger water supply, I could have resumed wasteful practices. But it's so easy to conserve water if you think carefully of your impact every time you want to use some.

For example, some standard advice is to make sure your washing machine contains a full load before running it. (Notice that this is the same advice for saving the energy it takes to run the washing machine. It's all connected.) Ditto for the dishwasher, if you choose to use one. But go beyond the standard advice and apply a little off-grid thinking: consider what constitutes a dirty dish. Certain dishes are not dirty just because they have been used once or twice. A glass that contained water can be used over and over before it needs the dishwasher treatment, or it can be subsequently saved to hold cranberry juice. Or vice versa. A knife that was used to cut a piece of fruit can be wiped off and kept around to cut another piece of fruit. I developed this theory in Taos when I did all my dishes by hand. When you rely solely on your own labor instead of a machine, you tend to redefine what it means to be clean. A lot of my off-grid conservation practices came about this way. A full year of practicing them made them habit.

In fact, one way to discover to what conservation lengths you are willing to go to is to experiment with this kind of off-grid thinking. Try buying five gallons of water at the grocery store and making it your only water supply for a weekend. Shut off the valve to the toilet, don't open any taps, and don't run any water-using appliances. How does your behavior change? Are you OK not bathing for two days, or do you take sponge baths or shower at the gym? Do you still use the same number of dishes, or do you consciously use fewer since you must wash them by hand? Have you resolved to put a brick in your toilet tank to reduce the amount of water used each flush? Did you hand-wash your lucky socks before going out Saturday night? Which of these behaviors can you continue on Monday when your "real" life begins again?

Be realistic. Shortly after moving back on the grid, I had a baby, which made it impossible to do laundry only once a month. So I conserve water in other ways and cut myself some slack on the baby's laundry, especially since I know this is a temporary condition.

Or be ambitious. If you want to take water conservation to an extreme, you can replace your flush toilets with composting ones that use no water whatsoever. In addition to conserving water, they make terrific conversation starters.

Don't confuse composting toilets with outhouses, although even those are a viable alternative for some, certainly if you live off the grid. In an outhouse, the toilet of choice all over Nepal, people deposit their waste in a hole and leave it to its own devices. Thus, outhouses can stink. (The big dilemma when using an outhouse in cold weather is whether to breathe through your nose. Breathing through your mouth is much more pleasant, but in cold weather, your nose tends to run. For me, it's always a race to see whether I can finish doing my business in time to step outside and inhale sharply through my nose before anything running out of it can pass my upper lip. Usually I forget and reflexively take a big sniff to stop my nose from running. Usually I regret it.)

A more abstract idea for water conservation is to share. For example, if you get rid of your lawn but crave

Marie's Composting Toilet

Before you conclude that outhouses and composting toilets are the provenance only of off-grid drop-outs, consider my friend Marie. I met Marie when I was working in the corporate world. At the time, she was launching her own business and working a part-time office job to help pay the bills. She also rented out half of the duplex she owned for some additional cash.

But Marie doesn't like to be dependent on anyone else, and she wanted to quit the office job, so she got creative. Taking stock of her assets, Marie figured that she could rent out both halves of her duplex if she had somewhere else to live. Applying some off-grid thinking, she decided that somewhere else was her own two-car garage.

Marie did her homework and decided that she could afford to remodel her garage into a livable space if she did the labor herself and made some unconventional decisions, such as not pulling a building permit since the garage wouldn't meet code in certain unnecessary (to Marie's way of thinking) ways. The biggest of these was not plumbing the garage. Marie installed a composting toilet, purchased her drinking water, and resolved to shower at the gym.

She bought the composting toilet on eBay, easily installed it herself, and used it regularly. When asked if she would do it again, Marie said yes, only that she would upgrade to a more efficient model.

Olive's Outhouse

When Olive first bought the shack, it included an outhouse located twenty yards away and in view of the front door. Not knowing how full the hole beneath it was and preferring a little privacy, she decided to move it to a less obtrusive location. She planted a couple of trees in the old location, one of them directly over the filled-in hole. It thrived, while the others withered.

Olive did not consider it a hardship not to have indoor plumbing. She simply stepped outdoors to her three-sided structure with panoramic scenery visible on the open fourth side. I used it one starry, starry night and marveled at the view that no other bathroom can boast.

some wide-open green space, go to a public park or golf course—essentially shared lawns. People love to decry golf courses as being environmentally insensitive. While it's true that monocultures (i.e., a single "crop," such as grass in this case) quash diversity both in plant and animal life, if we all xeriscaped our yards and left all-grass monocultures to parks and golf courses, it wouldn't be such a threat to the environment. Our backyards would promote diversity of species, and we could share the grassy spaces.

If you don't have a washing machine, do your laundry at a Laundromat and share their facilities, electricity, and water. Public pools constitute a shared use of water too. Having your children play in a public fountain (ordinances permitting, of course) is a different use of shared water, as opposed to running through a sprinkler at home. It's more social too.

All of these suggestions may strike some people as being too difficult, silly, unnecessary, or just plain weird. I maintain that these people are too absorbed in the details of their daily lives to be able to step back and view the entire picture. These people don't want to conserve; they prefer to perpetuate the status quo and let someone else solve their problems. (If you are not part of the solution . . .) This way of thinking (or failing to think, as the case may be) applies to every chapter in this book, but it will be felt soonest and most critically where water is concerned.

There is a pattern here. No matter the topic—pick any of these chapters—invariably I will read a sentence such as the following from the Colorado School of Mines' annual publication, *Energy and the Earth Global Research 2009*: "Although freshwater resources are completely allocated, population continues to grow and demand continues to rise. Meanwhile, uncertainties due to climate change create additional stress on available water resources. It's clear new approaches are needed."

What's clear to me is that population growth and demand increases are assumed to be givens rather than the root of the problem when the issue is approached in an on-grid way. The CSM publication goes on to discuss the fascinating research the college is doing in wastewater reclamation—worthwhile research for sure, but really only a band-aid on the true problem. On-grid thinking drives us to seek solutions that will allow us to continue our wasteful status quo. Let's use a little off-grid thinking to develop habits of conservation that will create a new status quo instead.

It's like applying for another credit card once your existing ones are maxed out. You can keep looking for money to borrow until you run out of lenders and are painfully forced to reduce your spending after it has become an entrenched habit, or you can reduce your spending immediately and develop new habits of your own accord. We have reached that point with water supplies in the American West and much of the rest of the country. With water, unlike energy, the problem is not in our children's or grandchildren's lifetimes; it's in ours. The conclusion is evident: either reduce our use voluntarily now or wait until supplies dry up and we are forced to.

The status quo where water is concerned will necessarily change in the near future. Whether we are prepared for it is up to us.

Food

*To forget how to dig the earth and tend the soil is to forget
ourselves.*

—Mohandas Gandhi

T HE FRONT ENTRY OF CID'S Food Market in Taos
has a wall-length bulletin board that locals use to
post notices. They range from fancy flyers with colored
photos promoting the coming weekend's latest bands to
handwritten sheets torn from spiral notebooks advertising
baby goats for sale. Whatever you are looking to sell, buy,
or experience, you can find it on this wall. Well drilling,
herbs for sale, belly dancing instruction, qigong classes,
roommates wanted, upcoming poetry slams, lost dogs, art
gallery openings, handymen available, group chanting,
fortunes made, fortunes told—you name it, it was there.

One day as I scanned the board on my way in, a photo
of a yurt caught my eye, as they aren't often found on
public bulletin boards. Beneath the photo, the advertiser

said he was looking for someone to work in his organic garden for the summer. In exchange, he would provide free lodging in the yurt on his property. If I didn't already have a place to live, I would have signed up for this deal. I don't have much of a green thumb, but I do possess a willing attitude and the desire to learn so I can grow some of my own food one day. And it would have been fun to live in a yurt for a summer.

WWOOFing

If you are interested in a hands-on opportunity to learn organic farming techniques, try WWOOFing. Willing Workers on Organic Farms (also known as World-Wide Opportunities on Organic Farms) is a global network of organizations that has been around since 1971.[28] You can participate as an organic farmer looking for extra help or as a willing worker looking for lodging. The idea is simple, as most brilliant ideas are. Small farmers get free labor in exchange for providing lodging, meals, and instruction. Workers, skilled or not, get a place to live and food for the summer, season, or the duration of their vacation, plus any knowledge they gain while there. Their only cost is transportation to the farm, orchard, or vineyard.

Maybe you want to learn organic farming basics so you can grow vegetables in your backyard. Maybe you want to expose your children to the real source of food. Or maybe you are looking for a different way to connect with the earth. Growing something with your own hands is a creative process and can be very satisfying. WWOOFing can help you do it.

Instead, I entered the store and bought the foodstuffs that I needed for the coming week. I would have to return in a couple of days for more fresh produce, but apart from that my shopping list covered breakfast, lunch, and dinner, and was meticulously planned for optimal use of leftovers, since I was trying to keep my costs down.

When I first moved to Taos and took stock of my bank account versus the high price of food at Cid's, the local organic grocery store, I had to rethink the way I ate. Having neither an income nor a microwave forced me to get creative if I wanted to avoid shopping at a chain supermarket. No more takeout three nights a week or big lunches out at work or even microwaveable frozen dinners. Instead, to save money, I took most of my meals at home and did the cooking myself.

Food consumption habits are integral to conservation practices in general. Food has a cost beyond its price tag: the environmental costs of pesticides and other chemicals, transporting it to our stores, and whatever packaging trash winds up in the local landfill.[29] It also affects our health. The food I ate and my conservation practices were definitely intertwined in my off-grid life, and the kind of food I bought was ideally organic and locally grown.

I quickly learned that planning meals, making prudent food purchases, and doing my own cooking had ramifications in areas of my life that I couldn't have predicted. Planning saved me money and eliminated wasted food. Making judicious purchases also saved money and reduced the amount of trash I produced. Cooking from scratch was healthier and reduced trash as well. The most surprising discovery, though, was that having to spend as much time as I did on food forced me to slow down and savor the whole process, which helped me de-stress from years of constant multitasking.

Some other discoveries followed. (I learned a lot about myself in my year off the grid.) Ironically, I already knew most of these revelations, but I had never had the time to put them into practice, being on the go so much.

First, I like to eat a big breakfast. It keeps me from getting hungry at ten o'clock in the morning and binging on junk food, which was my habit in the corporate world. I used to exercise several mornings before work, then grab a chocolate croissant and a glass of orange juice on the way to the office. In Taos, a typical breakfast consisted of yoghurt, fresh fruit, juice, tea, and some form of protein.

Without a microwave, I had to figure out what protein was easiest to prepare. The previous night's leftovers could be heated in the oven, but bacon and eggs made for some really dirty pans. Eventually I got into the habit of eating (organically raised, nitrate-free) bratwurst for protein because it was precooked and I could heat it simply by boiling it in a pot on the stove. All the pot needed was a quick rinse and a wipe-down for me to consider it clean.

As I write this in my current on-grid life, the eccentricities leap off the page. Now that modern American culture washes over me daily, I wonder that I ever lived without a microwave or subsisted on bratwurst. And I wonder why I care.

It took about an hour to prepare and eat breakfast, but since I didn't have a job, I could take my time. It was a relaxing start to each morning to sit outside and observe the world waking up. The sagebrush was quiet except for the wind or the occasional crow passing overhead. Afterward, I went to the pool for a swim.

The second thing I discovered was that it paid to keep on hand snacks that required no preparation. When I get hungry, I want to eat immediately, which makes me susceptible to eating whatever is available, healthy or not. I have also been known to drive into town specifically to buy a brownie. For healthy snacks, apples and cheese, vegetables and hummus, avocado and tomato with olive oil and sea salt, or nuts and dried fruit were easy favorites. With the exception of the oil, salt, and nuts, all of the ingredients were local and organic. I made a midafternoon ritual out of eating my snack while sitting on the couch with my feet up, staring out the window at the clouds and letting my mind wander. It was a nice twenty-minute break from whatever activity occupied me.

Third, meat is expensive, and I am cheap. But I love good food and didn't want to sacrifice taste or quality, so I came up with the following ways to economize and still eat healthy amounts of protein.

- Buy steak or other high-quality, expensive meats no more than once a month. Better yet, eat it only out at nice restaurants, of which Taos has plenty. They usually have the best grades of meat anyway.

- Buy lesser cuts of beef, such as stew meat, and learn to prepare them well.

- Buy expensive meat only on sale. Cid's has a freezer with marked-down meat they are trying to get rid of. I checked it out when my weekly menu called for red meat and came up with some bargains.

- Buy bone-in chicken thighs instead of boneless breasts. The former run less than $2 per pound, the latter sometimes $8 per pound. Cooking with the bone in adds flavor, and the methods you must employ ensure juicy tenderness. I will never cook with boneless chicken breasts again.

- Eat fish. It's good for you, cooks quickly, and can be had cheaply depending on the type you buy. Canned tuna counts as fish, and I make a mean tuna melt. However, I hated stinking up my house by cooking any other kind of fish, especially during the winter when I couldn't keep the windows open. Fish became another protein source I ate only at nice restaurants. The quality is usually guaranteed, and the preparation exceeds anything I can do at home.

- Skip the meat and eat legumes instead. A large percentage of the world's population gets complete protein through combining legumes and grains. Combinations could be prepared in the form of a pinto-bean-and-rice burrito, Cajun red beans and rice, or pasta with cannellini beans and pesto. Lentils and rice is another common pairing. Cid's carries canned Indian food, including several varieties of lentils in sauce that I could heat on the stovetop and serve over rice. This became a cheap and easy staple whenever I couldn't think of anything else to prepare.

- Eat eggs. They are the perfect little package of protein and can be prepared innumerable different ways: scrambled, fried, hard-boiled, baked, and poached. My Aunt Jan has perfected the art of poaching eggs, which she taught to me several years before I moved to Taos. But by the time I needed to poach an egg for a cheap, healthy dinner at my off-grid house, I had forgotten how. I had to call Aunt Jan and Uncle Alan for instructions. (Aunt Jan does the cooking; Uncle Alan loads the dishwasher and makes sure everyone's wineglass is full.)

Perfect Poached Eggs

The cooking process goes quickly, so prepare everything you need first. Set the table and pour the orange juice. Put the bread in the toaster (but don't toast it yet). Fill a saucepan with water and put it on the stove. Crack your eggs in a bowl and set it aside. Then bring the water to a boil in the saucepan. Once it boils, turn it down to a simmer and slide the eggs in. Aunt Jan's method is to swirl the water with a slotted spoon and slide the eggs in the direction of the swirl. Start the toaster. (You could also set a timer for three minutes at this point.) When the toast pops up, put it on the plate and butter it, taking your time. Then turn the stove off and remove the eggs with the slotted spoon so they drain. Set an egg or two atop each piece of toast. Sprinkle with salt and pepper.

Fourth, being cheap, I couldn't stand to waste food, so I consumed all of my leftovers. This required a lot of planning, if I wanted to do it well. Leftover meat from dinner could certainly be eaten at breakfast, no matter what it was, but it also made a terrific starting point for the next night's meal. Roast chicken could be shredded and tossed on a salad, rolled in enchiladas, or baked in a pot pie; the carcass could be boiled down for stock. A few bites of leftover steak could be heated in a cream sauce and served over a baked potato. Anything could be tossed into an omelet, soup, pasta dish, or risotto. Knowing some basic cooking techniques allowed me to prepare these last four dishes no matter what the specific ingredients were.

Great Dishes for Leftovers

One way to use less where food is concerned is to eat your leftovers. Whether they come from a restaurant or your own cooking, no matter if you eat them as-is or turn them into something else, eating your leftovers is an excellent way to practice thrift and conservation. The alternative, which I have done my share of, is to leave them in the fridge until they go bad and then throw them away. In Taos, with no fridge space to speak of, I relied on four main dishes to use up leftovers:

- omelets (or "scramblets" if you lack omelet-flipping skills as I do)

- risotto (my favorite dumping ground for leftovers)

- soup (use a canned soup as a base—Thai, vegetable, noodle—and add your leftovers to beef it up)

- pasta with leftovers

Fifth, any leftovers I could eat hot I could also eat cold. Food preparation takes a lot of time, and I am as lazy as I am cheap. Sometimes I just didn't feel like cooking or spending the money to go out. A little gastronomic fortitude and a dash of Sriracha sauce make anything palatable.

Sixth, there was an incentive that made me willing to spend a large portion of my time planning, shopping, and cooking: I had more time than money. In my previous existence, my situation was the opposite, as I suspect it is for most Americans. I spent so much time at work that I convinced myself I needed to compensate by filling my free time playing just as hard. I sacrificed sleep and relaxation, instead opting for high stress levels and conveniences such as takeout meals. Convenience comes with a price: monetary, environmental, and physical.

Having more time than money was the biggest incentive to rethink my entire eating strategy, because I couldn't simply buy my way out of the problem as I used to do. But I didn't need to. I found that I enjoyed sitting down with back issues of cooking magazines and coming up with a meal plan for the week, and that I wished I had chosen to slow down, put some hobbies on hold, and spend more time in the kitchen when I was working.

In Taos, with the luxury of not having a job, my life was stripped to its bare essentials. If you can while away your hours with no restrictions, you find out what your priorities are, and they might be different from what you tell yourself. Mine included spending time outdoors, but that could mean working in my garden or reading a book while sitting on a lawn chair eating homemade cookies. It didn't have to mean outdoor sports. Mine also included engaging in hands-on creative activities where I could see the results, such as gardening and cooking. It made me wonder why I had stayed so long in a routine that provided no such fulfillment.

Once I became good at it, weekly meal planning took not more than two hours each week, and that's only because I sipped a leisurely cup of tea while I reread the magazine articles, noting food trends from a decade ago and which exotic ingredients had become mainstream.

Shopping took another couple of hours per week, mostly because I typically went to the store twice. The size of the cooler limited the amount of food I could purchase, and I wanted my produce to be as fresh as possible anyway.

Cooking took the most time. Since my favorite part of the day is the morning, I liked to linger over making and eating breakfast. Lunch was more utilitarian—I just wanted to eat out of necessity and get back to what I was doing. Dinner was a different story.

My primary activities in the evening were making and eating dinner and cleaning up the day's dishes, followed by reading a book. It was a huge change from my previous life. Formerly, when I spent the bulk of my day working away from home, I had limited time in the evenings to do house projects; shop, cook, and eat; conduct my social life; and pursue my hobbies. If I wanted to cram everything in, I had to multitask: eat out with friends or on dates, have breakfast in the car on my way to work, grab a snack while doing chores, nuke a frozen dinner after coming home from skiing.

> *Convenience comes with a price: monetary, environmental, and physical.*

In Taos, I learned the art of slowing down. Each of the activities above deserved my full attention, especially if I wanted to do it well. Driving always deserves your full attention, but so does eating breakfast. By spending more time on making meals, I ensured the highest-quality ingredients went into my body, which improved my health. By giving myself time to savor it, I could appreciate the goodness of what Nature had to offer. It is also well known that good digestion starts in the mouth.

Eating slowly and chewing thoroughly allows your saliva to begin breaking food down. This doesn't happen when you stand over the kitchen sink and shovel an English muffin into your mouth while reading the morning paper—a former habit of mine when I wasn't chowing down chocolate croissants.

Even taking my time in the grocery store paid off. Not being in a rush allowed me to walk down every aisle, see what was on sale, and get ideas for the next week's meals. I had time to find the ripest peach, if they were in season, or the sweetest melon. I could compare prices, even if it meant breaking out a calculator to divide down to the per-ounce cost to find the true comparison. I weighed produce. I checked dates on the milk cartons. I read labels. Yes, I became that person.

Spending an hour or so in the grocery store saved me money. Not being in such a hurry all the time saved me stress—a huge health benefit on its own. Buying food in small amounts prevented it from going bad in my cupboard. And figuring out how to eat organic boosted not only my health, but the health of the planet as well.

Definition: Organic

According to the U.S. Department of Agriculture, to be certified organic, food production must avoid the use of most synthetic or chemical products (e.g., pesticides, fertilizers, additives, routine antibiotics, growth hormones), genetic modifications, irradiation processes, and the use of sewage sludge.[30] (It bothers me that any crops would be grown using sewage sludge, organic or not.) Standards exist for organic produce, dairy, meat, eggs, and wine, but not for fish.

The True Cost of Food

Food is the only area in which using fewer of the planet's resources might require you to spend more—at least if you judge its cost only by your grocery bill. But sometimes things are not what they seem, and assumptions lead you to the wrong conclusion.

I once biked up the road that leads to the Taos Ski Valley. This road climbs nearly two thousand vertical feet over seven miles. I took my time and stopped frequently to catch my breath, figuring that the work of going uphill was payment for the pleasure of rolling effortlessly the whole way down. What I didn't count on was how terrifying the descent was. Despite having just biked up it, I didn't seem to register how steep, narrow, and curvy the road was, and I gripped my brakes in fear the whole time.

I was thus suitably awed on a different occasion by the skinny, long-haired kid on a skateboard with no brakes who rolled down it. As I approached him from behind in my car, he fearlessly occupied the whole road, forcing me to slow down as he zigged and zagged in tight turns across both narrow lanes. When I had the opportunity to pass him, I did so cautiously and turned to give him a thumbs-up. That's when I noticed he must have been at least sixty years old.

So never take your assumptions to be fact before checking them out.

Most people assume they must pay more for organic food. It is true that your grocery bill will be higher at Cid's Food Market or Whole Foods than at your average grocery store or SuperTarget. Buying organic at the supermarket is cheaper than the natural food store yet still more expensive than if you filled your cart with frozen dinners, processed cereals, sweets, and treats.

There are environmental costs associated with "conventional" farming methods that don't appear in the sticker price.

But consider this: your health and that of the planet are tied to the quality of the food you buy and eat. There are environmental costs associated with "conventional" farming methods that don't appear in the sticker price.

"Conventional" Farming

The quotation marks are deliberate, because the word *conventional* makes no sense in its current usage. *Conventional* implies that these methods of farming are well established, when, in fact, they only became widespread after World War II when the chemicals developed for the war effort were repurposed as insecticides (think DDT) and fertilizers. Have you ever wondered why fertilizer is an ingredient in homemade bombs? Crops have only been grown drenched in chemicals on a large scale for less than one hundred years. Prior to that, all farmers were organic, even if no one called it that. The organic food movement is simply reclaiming the natural order of things.

The practice by large agribusiness to increase their crop yields through the use of chemical fertilizers and insecticides has depleted the soil of nutrients. At some point, the nutrient profile of the land will need to be rebuilt. For example, the soil will need to be replenished with nitrogen. There is a cost to this. There is an environmental cost to the use of all those chemicals as well. They linger on food, are ingested by insects and birds, and sometimes contaminate water supplies.

There are costs to your personal health too. If the soil doesn't contain nutrients, then neither does the food that grows in it. There is mounting evidence that organic foods are more nutrient dense than their "conventional" equivalents, particularly in terms of antioxidants, the compounds that will protect you from cancer and other diseases most prevalent in the developed world.

When you account for those issues, organic food looks cheap by comparison. Organic bananas are sixty-nine cents a pound. Coronary bypass surgery is thousands of dollars. That's a lot of bananas.

There are also agricultural vulnerabilities associated with "conventional" agribusiness practices. Agribusiness's tendency to grow a monoculture is inherently more prone to failure from pest infestation or crop blight than the variety of crops grown by small organic farmers. Just as with your financial portfolio, it pays to diversify.

Small farmers are more likely to grow heirloom produce—that is, varieties of produce that have been around for centuries. Agribusiness is more likely to grow few varieties based on how easy they are to produce, how well they travel, how they look on the shelf, how long they last—and how much profit they generate. Agribusiness thrives on economy of scale, but healthy soil and healthy bodies do not.

There are many reasons to buy organic, the most obvious of which is that it is better for you. "Conventionally" grown crops are laden with pesticides, none of which are necessary or beneficial to the human body—an understatement, since they are of course the opposite. If you wouldn't drink a bottle of weed killer, why would you ingest it along with your fruits and vegetables? Plus, organic food is better for the environment (i.e., neighboring plants and animals) not only by avoiding harmful pesticides and chemical fertilizers, but also by using less water and energy as well.

Most small farmers in the Taos area use organic methods. They sell their products at Cid's and at the farmers' market that is held every summer in a parking lot just off the downtown plaza. I like to while away a Saturday morning chatting with the farmers, ranchers, and beekeepers who set up booths there. They are typical Taos eccentrics, if atypical farmers. As one put it, the vegetables are chemical-free, but he can't vouch for the farmers.

Pesticide Residue on Fruits and Vegetables

According to the nonprofit organization Environmental Working Group, the following types of produce are the most and least likely to contain residues of the pesticides used when they are "conventionally" grown.[31]

Most Likely to Contain Pesticide Residue

apples	carrots	celery
cherries	imported grapes	kale
lettuce	nectarines	peaches
pears	strawberries	sweet bell peppers

Least Likely to Contain Pesticide Residue

asparagus	avocados	cabbage
eggplants	kiwis	mangoes
onions	papayas	pineapples
sweet corn (frozen)	sweet peas (frozen)	watermelons

This is the picture that enters my head when I think of organic farming, although I am aware that the big food manufacturers have gotten in on the action to take advantage of a growing trend. I am of two minds about this. While I worry that they may lobby for a looser definition of "organic," which would degrade its meaning, the advantage is that far more acreage is now under cultivation free of chemicals.

But I would still rather buy my food directly from the person who grew it, who lives up the road and is a member

> **Fact:**
>
> Small local ranchers and farmers may avoid pesti-
> cides, routine antibiotics, growth hormones, and
> chemical fertilizers, yet they still might not have
> an organic label. Getting certified by the USDA is
> expensive. Ask if they meet your criteria and buy
> locally if they do.

of my community. Their food is fresher, and therefore
more healthful (for myself and the planet) for not having been trucked a thousand miles to my supermarket. It
was picked a couple of days before I bought it, driven a
few miles to town, and handed to me in a brown paper
bag or simply placed in my reusable canvas shopping bag.
That's the lowest carbon footprint available for food short
of growing your own vegetables.

By contrast, organic food from big agribusiness travels across the country in a refrigerated truck so it can land
on the grocery store shelves packaged in plastic.

The ecological benefits of organic food are counter-
acted by the resources expended and pollution created to
ship it. If it actually comes from a different country, as
10 percent of organic food does, the cost to the planet is
higher than the costs mitigated by being grown organically.
It is always best to buy locally sourced organic foods.

Minimizing Your Food's Ecological Footprint

The gold standard for minimizing your ecological footprint from the food you eat is to obtain locally produced,
organic food. While that was easy for me to achieve while

Plastic Contamination of Food

What goes around comes around. Back in the '70s, when microwave ovens were first introduced, we worried about plastic leaching into our food when we heated it up. In the absence of hard evidence, we feared the newfangled devices would cause cancer or other diseases. Then convenience took over and we forgot to care. New evidence now supports the idea that plastic, specifically polycarbonates (often labeled with recycling code #7), contains Bisphenol A (BPA), which is a hormone disrupter. Other plastics, such as polypropylene (PP; recycling code #5) and polyvinyl chloride (PVC; recycling code #3), may also contain substances that can leach into food and wreak havoc in our bodies. So the advice from three decades ago applies again, with some additions:

- Always microwave your food in glass or ceramic, never in plastic, including the Styrofoam containers that sometimes serve as restaurant doggie bags.

- If you are particularly concerned, don't even use plastic storage containers or plastic wrap for food.

- Do not drink hot liquids from Styrofoam.

- Do not use cooking oils that are bottled in plastic. A better alternative is oils purchased and stored in glass bottles.

living in Taos, it was more difficult once I moved back on the grid in Colorado. My family now includes a husband and baby, which comes with conflicting priorities. On one hand, I am now even more concerned (or obsessed) with food. My daughter's health is a clean slate that I don't want to contaminate. On the other hand, I have far less time than I did as a single, unemployed person living off the grid. Planning weekly meals for a family isn't much harder than planning only for myself, if I can only find the time. I have reverted back to buying pre-prepared meals, this time from Whole Foods, when I am too occupied to cook my own.

But I still follow the guidelines I came up with in Taos for inexpensive protein sources. When I decided that poached eggs were fine for dinner, I had to call my aunt and uncle again to get the recipe.

"Are you calling to ask how to poach an egg?" Uncle Alan asked immediately upon answering the phone. I was flabbergasted at his prescience, but it turned out that he was halfway into a bottle of wine and remembered how funny it was when I called for the method several years prior.

Having reentered the mainstream, I now struggle with keeping my life as slow paced and stress-free as possible. I don't multitask; I'm bad at it anyway. I have given up most of my other activities in favor of taking care of my baby daughter. But I still yearn to connect with my natural surroundings and enjoy spending a large part of my day outside, which can be accomplished by pushing a stroller. And I continue to focus on a goal of minimizing my family's ecological footprint to maximize our health and that of our small corner of the planet. As food preparation once again dominates my free time, I have brainstormed three primary options for busy people to reduce our impact on the earth while maintaining good health.

First, we can grow our own.[32] This option provides the ultimate connection between humans and the land, one that we have lost but can easily reclaim if we are willing to give up a different priority to focus on it. Caring for my baby currently dominates my life, but I have big plans for the future when my daughter is a little more self-sufficient. It looks as though we will stay put for a while, so I have come up with a Grand Vision for our house here as well.

Our large backyard consists of an untamed slope with vast potential. There is room for fruit trees at the top by the street—maybe peach trees next to the existing apple trees. Right by the house, I can replace the nondescript bushes with fruit-bearing ones such as raspberry or blackberry. Over by the shed, there is a small, steeper pitch whose soil needs to be stabilized so it won't erode, and strawberry plants are a potential solution. Their roots weave into a mat as they grow and spread.

We already have three raised garden beds that the former owner of our house constructed. One of them receives full sunshine every day all summer long, which is perfect for many edible plants. Herbs are a great choice to grow yourself, because they tend to be expensive in the grocery store, and because you generally need only one tablespoon at a time, you end up discarding what's left of the precut store-bought herbs that go bad before you can use them.

The other two planters receive partial shade and can be used for plants we like to eat or which store well. My husband is fond of cucumbers and radishes, and you can't go wrong with tomatoes and hot peppers for fresh

Gardening with Limited Space

If you don't have a backyard or plot of ground to call your own, you can still grow some of your own food.

- Plant a single vegetable that is a prolific producer, such as certain varieties of cherry tomatoes or an herb like mint.

- Plant a mini vegetable garden in a single large pot. Choose combinations that you know you will eat frequently, such as tomatoes and basil for pasta, or tomatoes, cilantro, and peppers for salsa.

- Plant herbs in several small pots. All you need is a sunny windowsill.

- Go vertical. Plant herbs, lettuces, or microgreens for salad in a Woolly Pocket, a "pocket" of soil lined with a moisture barrier and designed to be hung on a wall.[33] Hang it outdoors if you have room, or on a sunny indoor wall instead.

- Join a community garden. Not only do community gardens beautify your area, they allow you to connect to the food you eat and the people and environment around you.[34]

salsa. Scallions, lettuce, carrots—we will experiment with whatever else strikes our fancy.

Ultimately, after my thumb becomes greener, I would like to install a greenhouse above the shed and the strawberry slope. During my year living in Taos, my neighbors Norbert and Shari built a greenhouse. That is, I eventually had to ask what the structure was that they had built, and they told me it was a greenhouse. Judging by the exterior, I never would have guessed.

I watched as it went up over the course of several weeks. It started as a giant frame of connected triangles, the lower ones supporting the upper ones in a matrix of stunted two-by-fours. The structure expanded into a large shell of a dome. I wondered if they were building an observatory, which would be a reasonable thing to do under the dark Taos night sky.

Their next step was to cover two-thirds of the frame with polyurethane spray foam and paint it with a pink-toned elastomeric coating. The wooden shell showed through enough to make it resemble a dimpled golf ball with part of its cover ripped off. The remaining third on the south side they covered in translucent Lascolite, which I mistook for Plexiglas. Probably not an observatory.

Eventually my curiosity got the best of me, and I had to ask. Upon finding out it was a greenhouse, Jason wondered if we could see inside.

"We're not growing pot in there," was Norbert's immediate answer.

But they did give us a tour. The interior was overgrown with fruit trees and multitudes of vegetables, plus some rosebushes and other decorative plants. Their theory was that it only paid to grow plants that were expensive to buy or that were difficult enough to obtain that they could sell them for a little extra cash. Norbert and Shari didn't grow cucumbers, no matter how much they liked them. Instead, they grew ginseng.

The greenhouse had another purpose as well. A walkway led invitingly from the entrance to a hot tub in the center. In the middle of winter, Norbert and Shari could take a relaxing soak while providing humidity for the plants. The whole construction was ingenious. Black plastic barrels the size of oil drums lined the interior walls on the north, east, and west sides. Norbert told us that they were the secret to a stable temperature inside the dome. In the winter, the sun poured through the translucent south side each day and struck the barrels, which were filled with water. They absorbed the heat because of their dark color and released it slowly overnight after the sun set. In the summer, the sun was too high in the sky to reach the barrels. The water inside them stayed cool and helped cool the greenhouse. Not only was it clever, it was cheaper than installing any kind of heating and cooling system. Norbert and Shari had taken advantage of passive solar principles to build a lush oasis in the middle of dry New Mexico.

When we finally build our own greenhouse up in Colorado, it may not contain a hot tub, but it will include a wall lined with black, water-filled barrels.

A second option for reducing your food-related ecological footprint is to shop at farmers' markets or community-supported agriculture cooperatives. If you don't have a green thumb or lack the space or time to grow your own food, a farmers' market is a local, typically organic way of having someone grow your produce for you. Golden, Colorado, where we live, has a thriving farmers' market every Saturday morning through the summer and into the fall. It's a social event for residents in addition to being a place to buy organic, sometimes locally grown produce. It's a cheaper alternative to organic grocery stores, and it's a way to help keep small producers in business. As with the farmers' market in Taos, it offers a wider variety of everything from tomatoes to potatoes, including some heirloom varieties that pack in more flavor than the standard supermarket choices.

There is something to be said too for witnessing the connection between food production and Nature. It may sound ridiculous, but when you shop only in grocery stores, you start to disassociate food from the earth that provides it. You may conclude that meat comes shrink-wrapped in plastic and vegetables arrive in frozen bags. Even fresh apples, when piled in an attractive display, are deceptively uniform. If you don't grow your own food, shopping at a farmers' market widens your experience to include the people who do.

Picking Apples

My friend Michelle picks fruit each summer and fall with her kids. There are farms and orchards all over Colorado that let you pick your own fruit. I went with her once to pick apples. We harvested one hundred pounds of apples in half an hour and had a lot of fun outdoors in the fresh air and sunshine doing it. Then we picked overripe peaches that were the last ones on the trees. Their skins were split open, and we could smell their juices baking in the sun. We had to swat the wasps away from the sticky fruit, but they didn't sting us because they were too busy gorging on the sugar. Michelle made applesauce, peach jam, and pie filling from our haul, some of which she froze for use in the winter. When she takes her kids on these excursions, it's entertainment for them as well as "grocery shopping" for the family and a learning experience to boot. Her kids learn that fruit grows on bushes and trees; it doesn't arrive at the supermarket from a laboratory (or, at least, it shouldn't).[35]

A different version of farmers' markets is Community Supported Agriculture (CSA).[36] These are programs that allow you to buy a share in a local farm, which gives you access to locally grown seasonal produce or whatever else the farm produces, such as eggs, meat, dairy products, honey, or even wine or fish. Some farms encourage you to visit them and witness their operation or participate in the harvest. Typically one person in the program serves as the collection and distribution point, traveling to the farm on a weekly basis to pick up whatever has been harvested.

CSA programs are cropping up all over. One of our neighbors in Golden is the distributor for a close-by, organic CSA farm. She has offered us samples of the fruits and vegetables they grow, and we are considering joining.

Community Roots in Boulder

One clever twist on CSA farms is the Community Roots organization in Boulder, Colorado. Created in 2006, the organization persuaded homeowners in a suburban subdivision to donate their yards and water to grow crops in exchange for a share in the harvest. Community Roots members provide the labor. Now that's some off-grid thinking. The benefits are many:

- Getting rid of useless, water-hogging lawns. (See how all the solutions fit together?)

- Growing food locally.

- Bartering labor and harvest for land and water (i.e., sharing resources).

- Healthy planet, healthy suburbs, healthy eating for participants.

A third option for reducing your food-related ecological footprint is to adopt a "flexitarian" way of eating,
as described in *The Flexitarian Diet* by Dawn Jackson Blatner.[37] This option is available to everyone, whether you
have or lack a garden, access to farmers' markets, or cooking skills. The fundamental idea is to reduce the amount
of meat you consume, replacing it with the other (notably
cheaper) sources of protein mentioned earlier.

Meat is expensive not only for your pocketbook but
also for the planet in terms of the resources required to
produce it. Livestock are responsible for a whopping 18
percent of greenhouse gas emissions around the globe.
Couple this with the resources necessary to grow their
food (land, water, and, if it's not organic, pesticides and
fertilizer), in addition to other forms of waste (such as
manure ponds) that come with the territory, and it is
clear that eating meat costs more to the planet than eating plant-based food.

If instead we eat lower down on the food chain, we
eliminate this waste and reduce our ecological footprint.
We also reap the health benefits that have been documented of a vegetarian diet. However, if you are like me
and can't give up a favorite meat (God bless the pig),
then adopting a "flexitarian" diet might be the answer.
It simply calls for being flexible in your protein sources
as I was in Taos. Start by eating a meatless meal once a
week, then twice a week, working up to whatever number of days seems achievable. Or eat meat only on special
occasions. Or follow the Chinese practice of eating the
protein mostly from sources with no legs (e.g., fish and
plants), less from sources with two legs (e.g., poultry),
and the least from sources with four legs (e.g., pork and
red meat). It is more healthful for you and gentler on the
earth. And it's cheaper.

When you start paying attention, you will notice that your goals converge. In Taos, living on savings, my primary incentive was to save money. I adopted a flexitarian diet before I knew what to call it, simply because my bank balance dropped with every purchase I made, no matter how small. I shopped at the farmers' market because the produce was fresher and more flavorful. Because it was seasonal, it was also cheaper. And because it cut out the middleman, it involved no packaging and minimal transportation, making it friendlier to the environment. I cooked most of my own meals at home to save money, which forced me to reprioritize how I spent my time.

Ultimately, the greatest benefits of the food practices I adopted in Taos were slowing down my life and establishing a stronger connection to the natural world, both of which can be achieved on the grid by anyone looking to improve their health and that of the planet.

☞ 6 ☜

Garbage

Waste is worse than loss. The time is coming when every person who lays claim to ability will keep the question of waste before him constantly. The scope of thrift is limitless.

—Thomas Edison

A T MY OFF-GRID HOUSE on our private road over the mesa, we had no trash service. Outside the house there was no nook containing heavy-duty plastic garbage cans that I could drag to the curb so the garbage company would haul away my waste without my having to make any further effort than writing them a check. I didn't even have a curb. The dirt road smoothed itself seamlessly into the sagebrush that lined its sides and threatened to reclaim it when I wasn't watching.

Inside the house things appeared more "normal." There was a tall garbage can in the kitchen and a small wastebasket in the bathroom. When the small one was full, I emptied it into the big one, but when the big one was full, I had a bag of trash and a problem.

As a homeowner, I was assessed a fifty-dollar quarterly fee for use of the county dump, so I could have taken my trash there, which I did for a while. But trash stinks. Taking it to the dump involved driving it there in my car. Not that I kept my car clean by any stretch—in the summer I habitually drove with the windows down and covered every surface with the fine dust kicked up from the dirt road, but dust doesn't have a lingering smell.

Also, sometimes trash is wet if you are not careful about what you put in the can. After my first experience with a leaking garbage bag in the back of my car, I double-bagged the trash every time I took it to the dump—a wasteful practice, and one that caused me to have to buy trash bags twice as often. The routine got old very quickly.

As with my other hands-on experiences in Taos, I realized that when I became directly involved in the things people take for granted on-grid (staying warm, using electricity, running water from a tap, and now removing trash), I came up with very different solutions to the problems. So I sat down and thought the problem through.

What, exactly, was my trash composed of?

- food containers: cans, bottles, cardboard, Styrofoam containers from restaurants

- food waste from meal preparation

- various packaging from the items necessary to run my house: toilet paper, cleaning products, personal hygiene items

I mentally sorted my garbage into several categories, each with a different disposal solution.

First and easiest, I had burnable items such as paper and cardboard. These went into the kindling bin. One advantage to a woodburning stove is that I could burn trash, assuming I felt like building a fire. Once in a while I built one to take the chill out of the air and to reduce the pile. A Boy Scout–worthy fire could be started with a pyramid constructed from cardboard paper towel and toilet paper tubes with crumpled paper underneath. I lit it with a long match and waited until the cardboard ignited in the flames from the paper and then gently laid on another pyramid of scrap wood. When it sufficiently held a flame, I added a log.

One Man's Trash Is Another Man's Treasure

My woodburning stove was itself somebody else's trash. Charlie bought it from a lady who had it for sale on a local radio program called *Trash and Treasures*. It had been stored in a shed, unused, ever since she inherited it when she bought her house. We bought it for two hundred dollars. Charlie had his crew clean it up and install a new stovepipe up to the ceiling. I loved its antique look much more than anything I had seen in the stores for sale new.

But there is a limit to what can be burned in the average household fire. The second type of trash was comprised of recyclable items; namely, plastic and glass containers and tin and aluminum cans. The majority of them came from the grocery store, and I rinsed them out and put them in a bag underneath the kitchen sink. When the bag was full, I would take it to the recycling center near the pool where I swam laps. Ironically, the year I lived in hippie-filled, tree-huggin' Taos, the recycling center did not accept plastic. I had to put my plastic containers in a large garbage bag and transport them to Colorado when I made a trip to visit friends.

Fact:

Plastic is a petroleum product.

The last type of trash was actual garbage that could not be burned, recycled, or reused in any way. It was almost exclusively food waste, with some product packaging as well. My goal became to reduce this third type.

I could look around my house and determine that I already had made decisions for other reasons that had the effect of reducing the trash I produced. I bought my drinking water in a refillable glass jug, for example, rather than in plastic bottles that would have to be recycled (and their caps discarded, as they are a type of plastic that is not recyclable). By not buying them, I lessened the demand for that plastic even to be created.

For health reasons, I preferred whole, natural foods that I brought home in a reusable canvas bag over manufactured "food" that came in a plastic tray sealed inside a plastic bag contained in a cardboard box. Again the solution to one conservation problem dovetailed with the solution to a separate problem.

Cid's Food Market

Whenever I went to Cid's, Taos's locally owned natural foods market, I took my own grocery bags—a practice that has gone mainstream. It eliminated paper and plastic bag waste and earned me poker chips, which could be put in containers at the front of the store that were labeled with the names of local charities and nonprofit organizations. Customers could choose which one they wanted to support and drop their chips in, and the store would make a corresponding donation. Customers who didn't bring their own bags received paper ones from the store. Used paper bags could be returned if they were in good condition, and the store passed them along to other customers.

Give a Hoot, Don't Pollute

Thirty years ago when I was a little girl, people routinely threw their trash out their car windows where it remained by the roadside and cluttered the landscape. The problem became so bad that an antilitter campaign was launched in response. It aired on TV in between Saturday morning cartoons: an animated owl exhorted us to "give a hoot, don't pollute." I must have internalized the message because it physically pains me to see manmade garbage in a natural setting. My house in Taos is nestled in the sagebrush and surrounded by mountains on every horizon. Trash has no place there. But I could make that case for any locale, whether it is wilderness, countryside, an urban center, or suburban sprawl.

The World's Highest Garbage Dump

Starting in 1953, when Sir Edmund Hillary and Sherpa Tenzing Norgay became the first people to summit Mount Everest, the world's highest mountain was on its way to becoming the world's highest garbage dump. Since that time, over four thousand climbers have followed, leaving behind fifty tons of trash, including empty oxygen bottles, discarded gear, wreckage of a helicopter, human waste, and an estimated 120 corpses. In the thin, dry air and freezing temperatures, garbage simply does not decompose. To compound the problem, climate change is causing the glaciers to recede, uncovering trash from Hillary's time that had been buried under the snow. It is ironic that in this remote region of the earth, inaccessible except to a miniscule fraction of the world's population, trash has become a pressing problem. On both the Nepalese and Tibetan sides, there are ongoing annual expeditions whose goal is to remove the refuse left behind by climbers and trekkers. The Nepalese government recently required a substantial deposit in addition to climbing fees in order to compel tourists to pack out what they pack in so that the mountain sacred to the local people can remain a pristine symbol of the wonder that is the natural world.[38]

Remember the United Nations statistic regarding our global collective ecological footprint of 1.4: it will take 1.4 earths to produce the resources we consume today and to render our waste harmless. Waste is part of the equation and needs to be taken as seriously as conservation.

But it's all connected. If you make your only goal creating less garbage, you will use less (and spend less) in all other categories in this book. Similarly, if you make spending less money your only goal, you will naturally conserve more of the earth's resources because you won't add to the demand for material goods and their packaging that is largely discarded.

> *If you make spending less money your only goal, you will naturally conserve more of the earth's resources.*

In Taos, I changed my consumption habits so that I made more recycling than trash. In fact, I wound up making so little trash—one small grocery bag's worth per week—that I simply threw it away when I bought gas rather than making an extra trip to the dump. But in Taos, I was motivated by having to haul my own trash, which is not the case for me back on the grid or any of us in a mainstream setting. I have a different incentive now.

Motivation comes in many forms. When I was in graduate school and living in a large complex of student housing, I had to carry my trash down three flights of stairs and across a yard to the Dumpsters. The college had a recycling program way back in 1993, so there were separate bins for plastic, cardboard, and three types of glass. (Before single-stream recycling, you had to sort out clear, green, and brown.) Because it was there and I was carrying loads anyway, I started recycling. The college had made it easy, which was enough of an incentive.

When I moved to Colorado Springs after graduate school, curbside recycling (disappointingly) did not exist. But because it had become part of my ethic, I couldn't bear to throw away anything that I knew could be productively recycled. Instead, I saved my glass, plastic, cardboard, and paper in the garage and looked up the nearest facilities that would take them. Every couple of months I loaded my car and made a trip. It wasn't difficult, but it did require ample storage space and a healthy commitment. Because recycling had become part of my consciousness, I had the commitment. Most people don't. They don't have the proper incentive.

Unless it is painless (e.g., your waste management company provides bins and curbside, single-stream pickup), most Americans won't recycle.[39] If you have to sort it, transport it yourself, or (my personal favorite), pay "too much" to have it hauled away, it doesn't seem worth it. Are we simply lazy? Or do we not care? I admit to being lazy, but I do care, a fact that I attribute to spending the bulk of my free time outdoors in appreciation of the earth and the sky and everything in between.

My college roommate moved from the East Coast to the West Coast and picked up a recycling habit along the way. She was therefore shocked when she went back East and attended a big party thrown by a friend. At the end of the party, my roommate asked her friend if she needed help taking the beer and wine bottles to be recycled. The friend said no, that was too much trouble, she was just going to set them out with the trash. My roommate was dumbstruck.

When she told me this story, I was stunned as well. To my way of thinking, having a party that generates several months' worth of recyclable material in one night is the perfect opportunity to start recycling if you don't already do it or even just to make a one-time effort. I could imagine the visual impact the mountain of used bottles would make when piled in a landfill—or this person's living room. But instead of seizing the opportunity, she let it slip away.

Fact:

New glass made with recycled glass (versus silica) saves on raw materials and energy. However, it is preferable to reuse glass containers rather than recycle them.

Maybe she wasn't being lazy or apathetic. Maybe she felt she couldn't be bothered to recycle because she had more important things to do. Maybe she didn't understand the impact of her behavior or how easy and vitally important recycling is. She clearly didn't have any incentive.

One way to see the importance of reducing the waste you create is to connect more fully with the earth itself. Spend time outdoors observing your surroundings—smell the flowers, cast your eyes on all living green things, listen to the birds and other sounds Nature produces. You can do this in a public park, on a hiking trail through the woods, or sitting on a lawn chair in your own backyard.

Now imagine having to pile all the trash you made next to that lawn chair, or on the side of that trail through the woods, or in the middle of the park. Would you make less of it? What's the difference between that and putting it in a landfill? What did the landscape look like before the landfill was there?

In Taos I could have piled my trash on my own property, but the idea of creating such an eyesore in a beautiful location galled me. My only other option was to haul my own trash, which motivated me to make less of it.

Back on the grid, we pay the waste management company to cart our trash away, like virtually everyone else in this country. There is no incentive to make less trash. In fact, the opposite is true: the path of least resistance is to throw things away, and that becomes the de facto behavior. We rely on people's consciences to not be wasteful, an unreliable incentive at best.

Grocery Bags in Norway

When I visited my brother Jan, who lives in Oslo, I made a trip to the local grocery store. I bought only what I could comfortably carry home since I had walked there. When the lady at the register totaled everything up, she asked me a question in Norwegian. Since neither of us spoke the other's language, it took a minute of gesticulating before I understood she was asking me how many plastic bags I wanted to purchase since I had failed to bring my own. Having to pay for bags here at home would cure me of being too lazy to retrieve them from the car when I have reached the store entrance and realized that I've left them behind.

Other countries do it differently. Germany passed the Recycling and Waste Act in 1996, which was aimed at manufacturers rather than consumers.[40] The goal is twofold: avoid creating waste in the first place (meaning when developing and manufacturing a product and its packaging) and recycle an item before disposing of it if possible. The result is that in 2007, more than 88 percent of Germany's packaging was recovered rather than disposed of. (By comparison, only 43 percent of similar packaging was recovered in the United States that year.) Not only was waste kept out of landfills, but Germany estimates it avoided the creation of 1.4 million tons of CO_2 emissions. Not too shabby.

Even though the laws are not aimed at consumers, German citizens have one of the highest recycling rates in Europe, at around 70 percent. (Here in America, we hover around 33 percent. We are world leaders in wastefulness.) But Germany makes it easy for its citizens to recycle at home and in public, where color-coded receptacles exist for glass, paper, cardboard, packaging, and even food and other biowaste. It makes no difference in effort to throw trash in one container or another, so the habit of recycling is an easy one to get into.

If we had similar receptacles in this country, it would be just as easy. Why not put them at every public park, stadium, parking lot, and downtown area where people congregate? Think big.

Fact:

Golden, Colorado, has just installed recycle bins in its downtown area right next to the trash cans.

Or think small. Small changes sometimes have the biggest impact. For example, how about three bins in the kitchen—one each for trash, recyclables, and compostables—instead of one? If your recycling bin is in the garage or is an unsightly mess in the corner of the kitchen, it won't achieve the same easy status as the trash can. Those of us who are lazy at heart will throw the odd bottle or can away just to avoid taking an extra step.

On-Grid Reality

Back on the grid, I slip into more wasteful habits. I have a baby and all the stuff that seems to come with her whether I buy it or receive it as a gift or hand-me-down. Our living room houses her latest toys, whose number we desperately try to keep down by quickly passing them along to friends after our daughter has outgrown them. Even so, boxes arrive at Christmas, birthdays, and any other holiday where social conventions require a present. We recycle the cardboard but dispose of plastic wrap. I cut tags from new clothes and carefully recycle the paper part while discarding the plastic fasteners. Every time I reach for the trash can, I consciously ask myself whether I can do something else with the item I want to get rid of.

The biggest concession I made in terms of trash was to use disposable diapers. It was a gut-wrenching decision. We all know that disposable diapers sit forever in a landfill, especially if they have been balled up tightly and shoved into the plastic tube that is the miracle of the Diaper Genie. We have one. It makes changing diapers easy, odorless, and convenient.

And there's the rub. My biggest problem is lack of time, as every new parent can attest to. But even without children, we all seem to be overscheduled, overworked, and overwrought. Stressed out, in other words. We don't seem to have time to cook from scratch, sort our trash, compost our kitchen waste, grow our own tomatoes, or change a baby in cloth diapers. We (myself included) look for convenience to save ourselves time.

Convenience products cater to people who can't employ a more labor- or time-intensive solution. The cost is reflected in the price, but there is an environmental price tag as well. Every time you throw away a disposable razor or a single-use cleaning towel (or diaper), you add to the planet's garbage woes. You contribute to the 1.4 earths it will take to produce the resources and absorb the waste. I am guilty too. I rationalize the diaper decision in two ways: it is one of the few areas of my life where I create excessive waste, and my use of disposable diapers is temporary.

Fact:

In 2006, Americans generated 251 million tons of trash, according to the Environmental Protection Agency, more than half of which came from residential sources.[41]

To me, this is different than purchasing endless cases of bottled drinking water that come shrink-wrapped in nonrecyclable plastic. One day my baby will stop using diapers; we never stop drinking water. I could not in good conscience buy our drinking water in small plastic bottles, but my conscience does allow for disposable diapers.

The real point is that every decision we make in our small house takes some thought, if only to fend off the clutter. With conscious, deliberate decision making, we have managed to keep our ecological footprint small enough that it allows for the temporary wastefulness of using disposable diapers.

Deliberate decision-making takes time too; it requires you to slow down and think. Sometimes the decisions themselves result in you having to slow down as well. And sometimes when you think about them, the amount of time a convenience product saves is ridiculously miniscule. How much time does it take to put a new blade in a razor versus throwing away the disposable one and grabbing a new one? Thirty seconds? What about rinsing out a cleaning rag and throwing it in the laundry versus discarding your Swiffer cover? One minute?

Cooking from scratch takes quite a bit more time than heating up a frozen dinner, but the personal and planetary health benefits are numerous (see chapter 5, Food). I happen to enjoy cooking, but I learned to enjoy it by doing it, and now I count it as a hobby. However, if I spend my time cooking, I am not spending it doing other hobbies than I used to pursue. These days, I have dropped a lot of former hobbies, as the baby has forced me to realign my priorities. I find that I don't care.

A typical on-grid day is largely occupied by feeding, changing, and cleaning up after our daughter. I also prepare meals for the adults in the house, and roughly once a week I find time to take a shower. It is as much a simple, bare-bones life as the one I lived in Taos, but in a different way. On nice days, I take my daughter outside and let her touch the bark on the trees or feel the texture of different leaves. She likes to examine the gravel and pick the grass and listen to the birds squabbling inside a neighboring bush. We can while away an hour like this. It's far more important than hurrying to a mommy-and-baby yoga class or carting her through the drugstore to buy more plastic convenience gadgets.

But you don't need a child to reorganize your priorities. You just need to realize that haste makes waste, as the saying goes. If you slow down and think carefully about the impact your actions have on the earth, your priorities will reorganize themselves. You might find your stress levels dropping as you eliminate extraneous, purposeless activities from your life.

If you slow down and think carefully about the impact your actions have on the earth, your priorities will reorganize themselves.

For example, whenever I cook, I ask myself what to do with each item as I finish with it. Over time, a pattern emerges and my behavior changes. For breakfast, I have yoghurt with fruit and granola. I eat enough yoghurt that buying it in individual serving containers makes no sense either financially or in terms of the resultant waste. So I buy it in large plastic tubs that can be recycled (or reused as handy storage containers so I don't have to buy those either). My only flavor choices are plain or vanilla, so that's what I eat. I don't miss the fruit flavors.

I used to buy granola that came in a sealed plastic bag inside a cardboard box. The box can be recycled, but the bag must be thrown away, so I switched to buying granola in bulk. The only bag involved is a plastic one that I store under the sink when I finish with it so I can take it to our local dog park to be reused. Finally, I buy whatever fresh fruit is in season (it's cheapest that way) and then toss the rinds or stems into a tub in the freezer to take it out to the compost bin later.

World War II Conservation Ethic

Once upon a time, our whole country knew how to reuse and recycle for the greater good. My mother and her friends were only little girls during World War II, but the conservation ethic that defined the war era lingers for them. My mother saves and reuses everything from plastic bags to paper towels that have been used only to wipe up water. She dries them out and uses them again—and why not? Her friend Cricket is a farmer and rancher who still maintains a Victory garden, although today it's simply called a garden. And her friend Betty composts her kitchen scraps, which is all the more admirable because Betty lives in a condo in Florida where she has neither a composter nor a yard in which to use it; she saves her scraps in her freezer to give to a friend with a garden.

Ironically, when I lived off the grid on two acres of land, I didn't compost. This was largely out of the fear of attracting even more rodents toward my house since I already had a mouse problem. I didn't want to add rats to the mix.

But back on the grid, it's different. Our neighbors have a compost bin at the corner of their backyard that we can access from ours. It is a simple hand-built wooden bin, rather than a fancy plastic one that would have cost them more. They let us add our compostable scraps to it in exchange for a little labor. Our neighbors are a retired older couple who are getting to the point that they don't want to turn over their heavy compost with a pitchfork anymore. My husband does it instead, and they let us use the compost on our garden. Sharing like this is a time-honored way to reduce your ecological footprint. [42]

The alternative would be that we all threw our kitchen scraps away and then bought bags of compost at the garden center every spring. Or we could each have our own compost bin and do our own labor. But there is no reason to insist on individual solutions when collaboration makes more sense. We connect as neighbors.

Imagine what we could achieve if we extrapolated this kind of thinking to our country or the planet as a whole.

Between the composting, recycling, and judicious purchasing (or lack thereof), I once again minimize the amount of actual trash produced each week. Once we are done with diapers, our family will produce one thirteen-gallon bag of trash per week, roughly the same amount of recycling, plus that amount again of compost scraps.

It might seem absurd to think so hard about what goes in the trash can, but it's all connected and every little bit counts. With this one small set of conscious decision-making, we are putting into practice the concepts of reduce, reuse, and recycle every time we eat breakfast.

Reduce, Reuse, Recycle

When you think about it, reduce, reuse, recycle boils down to just two concepts: reduce and reuse. Recycling is simply donating your materials so someone else can reuse them. While reducing the amount of waste you produce is important, equally so is finding creative ways to reuse items that might otherwise become trash. Taking bags to the dog park or using empty toilet paper rolls as kindling are two examples.

Another obvious example is to fill your material needs with secondhand goods. In plain English, shop at garage or rummage sales. Personally, I hate shopping, especially for clothes. When I still worked in the corporate world, I had to dress the part, but I increasingly resented spending my hard-earned money on clothes for a job I found unfulfilling. It was a slap in the face every time I laid down a credit card to buy an outfit I didn't want to wear so I could conform to the standards of a company I didn't want to work for. So it was a godsend when a friend turned me on to an annual rummage sale in one of Colorado's mountain towns.

The Minturn Annual Rummage Sale is held every August at the town of Minturn's middle school. It is comprised of room after room of donated clothes, household goods, baby items, books, artwork, sports gear, and even furniture. The proceeds go to local police, fire, ambulance, and search-and-rescue organizations, and the event is staffed by their members. Prices are set at standard rummage sale levels—I bought a pair of unused skis for twenty dollars rather than for four hundred in a retail store—but the quality of the goods is markedly higher than what I have encountered elsewhere.

The reason is that Minturn is located in the Vail Valley and is surrounded by ritzy ski towns. The good people of the Vail Valley donate their castoffs throughout the year, and frugal folk like me shop each fall for name-brand clothes to wear to work. I have bought Icelandic sweaters for fifty cents and Ferragamo shoes, very lightly used, for four dollars. (Before the Minturn rummage sale, I had never heard of Ferragamos and didn't know how expensive they were. My sister, who was with me that year and found the pair in my size, told me that she had paid two hundred dollars for a new pair for herself. It had never occurred to me that any pair of shoes could cost two hundred dollars.)

After I discovered the Minturn rummage sale, I limited my clothes shopping to once a year. I much preferred to spend my money on clothes that already had a sunk cost where the environment was concerned (that occurred when they were originally manufactured and can't be recovered) and where my money would go to help some worthy organizations. Also, the atmosphere there is that of a big, backyard party. Behind the school there is a grill where they sell hot dogs and hamburgers, or you can get a brownie or cookie at the bake sale. All proceeds of everything go to the same organizations. It was a much more entertaining and satisfying experience than spending a Saturday afternoon at a mall paying inflated prices for new items that had environmental costs I couldn't stomach. Especially when I preferred to spend my Saturday afternoons enjoying Nature, not plundering her.

You don't need a Minturn rummage sale to buy expensive items at fire-sale prices. Simply go to the expensive neighborhoods wherever you live and wander through their garage sales. The pickings are just as good.

A less obvious example of reusing castoff materials can be found at the Greater World Earthship Community just outside of Taos. When you drive west over the Rio Grande Gorge Bridge, the road makes a wide arc to the north, just after which is a small settlement of buildings crouched under the arching sky. You must look carefully to notice them because they blend into the rolling landscape. Each house has an earth-bermed north wall and an expanse of glass on the south side that is angled up toward the sun. They are long and low, curvaceous and earth-toned. These are Earthships.

Earthships are some of the greenest modern houses on the planet. They are quite literally built out of trash, their primary building materials being rammed earth encased in old tires (for load-bearing walls) and aluminum cans or bottles in a cement matrix (for nonstructural walls). The building materials were chosen out of respect for the earth and share certain qualities. First, they are indigenous materials, which contributes to the sustainability of the Earthships, rather than manufactured materials that must be transported to the building site. (It is ironic that garbage can now be considered indigenous, but it does fit the definition.) The rammed earth and concrete walls provide thermal mass, and the Earthships are durable and resilient and can be obtained and worked on by anyone with any skill level. Thus Earthships are accessible to anyone who wants to build a sustainable house with their own hands.[43]

If more houses were built using Earthship principles, or if more decisions were made using such careful reasoning, it could help "render waste harmless"—perhaps enough to lower our collective ecological footprint below 1.0 and make our way of life truly sustainable.[44]

The most creative example I have found for reusing waste materials is to transform them into art. Taos is populated by artists of every stripe, and I had only started to dip my toe into the art scene by the time I had to leave. My tour guide was my neighbor Olive, who makes jewelry out of "found objects." In other words, out of discarded stuff.[45]

Olive's Jewelry

My neighbor Olive earns her living as a jewelry maker. Her work combines elements of silver, copper, enamel, wood, watercolor, colored pencil, paper, textiles, resin, and found objects fabricated and assembled in a collage-like style. She sees jewelry as wearable art and finds the art-versus-craft debate terribly boring and rather silly. Olive finds inspiration in hardware stores as well as toy shops and flea markets and, of course, by traveling and seeing old things with new eyes.

Once I started to explore the art world, especially in connection with sustainable practices, I discovered the quirky niche of trash art. If you do a quick online search of the phrase *trash art*, you will come upon thousands of links to imaginative uses for trash. Some of my favorites are compiled on the Webdesigner Depot website, where they describe the use of trash and found objects to create art as "upcycling." (They are creating a new vocabulary too.)[46]

Some of the art in question looks literally like piles of garbage until a spotlight trained on one side projects the pile's shadow onto a wall where it is transformed into recognizable silhouettes: a man with a top hat and cane, a motorcycle, two people sitting back to back, a city skyline. Another sculptor uses old car parts and recycled metal to create sculptures of a flying pig, a classical male nude torso, and a television (to illustrate that there is "a lot of rubbish on TV"). Yet another artist upcycles junk into celebrity portraits and even an impressive version of Monet's water lilies.

I may not be as creative as these artists, but their work inspires me enough to hold on to my collection of old skis so I can turn them into a chair someday.

There was another commercial that was broadcast during Saturday morning cartoons in the '70s. In it, a Native American stood on a bluff overlooking a river. Trash lined its banks, and the whole scene was gray and dismal. The commercial ended with a shot of the Native American's despondent face, a single tear rolling down his cheek as he surveyed the desecration of the landscape.

Whenever I encounter a pristine natural setting, such as the top of a mountain or a flower-filled meadow tucked away in the thick of a forest, and I come upon a piece of manmade trash, I have the same reaction. Tin cans, plastic bottles, scraps of paper, lost hiking gear—I have seen it all, and it makes me sad. I think it is a common sentiment that manmade trash is out of place in such settings because they show no other signs of any manmade intrusions and feel like sacred ground. But trash is out of place everywhere, even in the middle of a paved Walmart parking lot. Despite the obvious human footprint, it's all sacred ground.[47]

Transportation

*The machine does not isolate man from the great problems
of Nature but plunges him more deeply into them.*

—Antoine de Saint-Exupéry

I T IS DIFFICULT TO FIND perfect silence. Getting
away from people helps but doesn't automatically produce stillness. The middle of a forest is a noisy place, for
example, with squirrels chattering and birds calling to
each other. The vacant top of a mountain seems like it
should be silent, but it usually has wind—sometimes a
very strong wind—blowing steadily or gusting.

Occasionally I have found myself alone on a moun-
tainside when the wind has died down. I have stopped,
listened, and looked around. The stillness is as vast and
imposing as the scenery. Virtually no animals live above
tree line, leaving only me and the view: usually line upon
line of more mountains, extending to the horizon. There
is a nobility in the silence that goes with the majesty of
the mountains. It bestows the ultimate sense of peace.

When I trekked in the mountains of Nepal, the scenery was so grand that the living creatures seemed to hush themselves in reverence. In a teahouse in one of the tiny villages on the way toward Everest Base Camp, I sat alone waiting for my lunch to be served. The porters had gone outside, and the entire village was quiet. The room was still as I looked at the photographs on the walls, pictures of climbers and trekkers frozen in time, colors fading, nearly everyone squinting into the harsh sunlight. I stepped carefully, not wanting to disturb the church-like quiet. But as I listened, I could swear I heard a faint, rhythmic thumping. It persisted as my soup arrived and continued after I had finished it. My guide came back, and I asked if he could hear it.

"Yes," he said. "This village has an old temple that is not active. No more monks live there. But once a month, one of the monks from the next village over walks up here to pray and chant with the villagers. He is beating a drum."

The only sound to break the stillness of the Himalayas that afternoon was a lone monk presiding over a decaying temple. As manmade noises go, it complemented the silence rather than intruded on it.

In the sagebrush outside Taos there are many opportunities for silence. With no trees, there are no clusters of songbirds—Nature's most consistent creators of background noise. I have stood outside in the post-rain dusk when the air has been freshly washed by the showers. You can almost taste it when you breathe it in, an idea which is enhanced by the sweet smell of wet sagebrush. The earth has just had a bath and is ready to go to bed. A few birds chirp intermittently, tucking themselves in for the night. They take turns speaking. There is no chorus.

There are no other sounds. The other animals out here don't make much noise around that time of evening. The hunters are quiet when stalking their prey, and the hunted are silently listening for the predators.

It is silent early in the morning as well before the wind picks up. As long as it is before or after Taos's meager rush hour, I can enjoy perfect quiet. My house is located a mile from the nearest road with any sort of traffic. When the wind is blowing, I can see but not hear the cars. But if any big trucks rumble by during my favorite early morning hours, their sound disrupts the tranquility. Traffic noise travels far. One of my most anticipated benefits to electric cars when they finally become commercially viable is that they make very little sound, noise being an overlooked form of pollution when we consider reasons to stop using fossil fuels. The other disadvantages to automobiles are obvious: air pollution; consumption of a finite resource (oil); reliance on foreign nations to provide that resource; potential for oil spills to contaminate coastlines, ocean waters, and other pristine environments; disruption of ecosystems and wildlife habitats when extracting oil. We have all heard of these. Noise pollution gets lost in . . . the noise.

There is yet another even more pernicious disadvantage to driving a car. It isolates you from your surroundings, contributing to one of the worst errors of thinking of modern civilization: that we exist apart from Nature. Our true role is as a part *of* Nature, which can only be fully realized if we slow down enough to be aware of our surroundings. If you never walk anywhere but rather always hurtle past at sixty miles per hour, you fail to notice the gifts that Nature has thrown in your path. Cactus that bloom for only a day or two. Birds engaged in courtship rituals. Camouflaged animals blending in with the rocks and plants.

One pernicious disadvantage to driving a car is that it isolates you from your surroundings, contributing to one of the worst errors of thinking of modern civilization: that we exist apart from Nature.

I noticed all these and other interesting subtleties in Taos as I took a daily stroll up the dusty double track and around Olive's shack. It was an unhurried part of each day that allowed me to stay in touch with the particulars of my habitat. Early summer blue flax gives way by July to high summer sunflowers that can withstand the heat. In September and October, tarantulas migrate to find mates. The sun sets a brilliant pink on the snows of Wheeler Peak in the winter. And the phoebes return in the spring to sit on the corners of my roof and whistle at me.

If I kept my head down as I went from my house to my car to an office and back again, living my life largely indoors as I did for years in the corporate world, I would miss out on all these phenomena and would remain oblivious to the mysteries of the universe. Instead, in Taos, I stayed mostly at home and spent the bulk of my time outside. When your feet touch the earth, they regenerate the connection that we are all born with.

This is not to say I didn't drive. In fact, the least environmentally friendly thing I did in Taos was drive a car. My transportation problem was essentially twofold: I had short-distance driving needs, such as getting to the grocery store or the ski valley from my house, as well as long-distance ones.

Carbon Footprint for Driving between New Mexico and Colorado

It is embarrassing to admit that my driving habits emitted roughly twenty thousand pounds of CO_2 into the atmosphere the year I lived off the grid. That more than offsets the carbon I saved by living a minimal-impact lifestyle.

When I moved into my house full-time, I anticipated driving a lot over long distances to maintain ties between my new home in New Mexico and Colorado where my friends and family lived. This was especially true during the winter since my ski buddies lived in Colorado. Throw in traveling for Christmas, and it was at least one trip per month from December to April. That's a lot of road trips. Eventually they wore on me, and I just wanted to stay put.

Whenever I was at my house, I did stay put. During the winter, if it snowed too much, I couldn't go anywhere because nobody plowed our road, and I was too cheap to hire someone. But as I didn't have anywhere pressing to go, I spent the time on my window bench with a cup of tea in my hand, watching the other inhabitants of the sagebrush.

Spring brought mud season, which lasts from March sometimes through June. The thick clay soil that serves admirably as home-building material turned into a gloppy mess after too much rain, gunking up your tires. I stayed put on those days too.

Even in summer and fall, the two car-friendliest seasons, I didn't drive into town every day, preferring to save my errands and run them all at once. It showed in my gasoline budget. In 2006 and 2007, gas prices had just started their steep ascent that would crest over four dollars per gallon in 2008. Living on savings, I was acutely aware of how much driving impacted my bank account. Without an income, it kept dropping regardless, but driving too much affected the rate at which it dropped, and driving was something entirely under my control.

Gas and Groceries

The two items left out of the most common Consumer Price Index inflation calculations are the two most volatile items in people's budgets. According to the Department of Labor, the average American household spends about 13 percent of their income on food and about 4 percent on gas. (These statistics reflect peak pump prices in 2008.) Fortunately, consumption of both items is firmly under your control.

Despite my conservation efforts, I drove a lot anyway. And it bothered me. I thought long and hard about the environmental impact of my driving and pondered how I could reduce it without too much of a sacrifice on my part. I needed to visit my friends. I needed a car to get to the ski valley since there is no public transportation to that destination. I needed to drive a lot of places.

I considered forgiving myself for being wasteful in that part of my life since I had such a small ecological footprint in all other areas, but driving makes a disproportionately large contribution to anyone's footprint. Aside from airplane travel, driving is the worst environmental crime you can commit. Besides, something still nagged at me, and I finally decided it was my attitude. Above, I said I *needed* to drive a lot of places. I use the word *need* several times, and in no case does it truly reflect what my transportation needs were. It also gives no clue to solutions other than hopping in a car.

My short-term "needs" really only included trips to the grocery store and occasionally to the recycling center. Every other destination—ski valley, swimming pool to work out, restaurants, Internet cafés—was a bonus. I didn't need to ski. I didn't need to swim to get a workout. I didn't need to check email or go out to eat at all. The long-distance "needs" could also have been eliminated with no real pain on my part, and I could have figured out transportation solutions that didn't involve driving my car.

American Car Culture

We have a tremendous sense of entitlement in America where cars are concerned, myself included. We feel entitled to own at least one car per person and to drive it as much as we please, the only constraint being whether we can afford the price of gas. Our cars have expanded their size, and our status and self-worth are wrapped up in them. Our cities are laid out to accommodate cars rather than pedestrians. We complain when there are too many potholes or when a road is closed for repaving. We grumble about our lengthy commutes, we whine about traffic congestion, we gripe about lack of parking, and we protest price increases at the pump.

Hitchhiking on the Mesa

There are people who lived farther out on the mesa than I did who didn't drive at all, whether by choice or necessity I am not sure. Yet despite being so remote, they seemed to live well enough without a car. Instead, they hitchhiked into town once a week to buy supplies, shower at the gym, and maybe go for some entertainment. I passed them all the time on a particular corner as they thumbed a ride back to their homes. Part of me wanted to pick someone up just to meet them and see what their life was like, but my house was only a couple of miles from their favorite corner so I wouldn't have had much of a ride to offer them. And I had watched too many movies involving hitchhikers.

But we never consider our contribution to the problems or question our right to drive wherever, whenever, and however much we please.

This psychology started during the Industrial Revolution, as we invented more and more machines to save ourselves labor. Pleased with the results, we developed the idea that machines were the key to less work and more leisure. With the invention of the internal combustion engine and the automobile in the late 1800s, we were suddenly mobile, off and running to explore and conquer the natural world. Adopting an antagonistic stance of man versus Nature was part of the package.

Fast-forward one hundred–plus years. Now, having emerged as the victors, we observe the natural world through the car window, exposing ourselves to the fresh air only long enough to roll it down and throw our gum

America's Mountain

In his book *Desert Solitaire*, Edward Abbey bemoans increased road access in national parks.[48] Since its publication in 1968, more pristine wilderness inside and outside the parks has seen road development. In fact, Pikes Peak in Colorado, known as America's Mountain, has a road all the way to its 14,115-foot summit. Purists like Abbey assert that the only people who deserve the panoramic views from the top are the ones who have reached it under their own power. I disagree, sort of. Colorado has over fifty other mountains above 14,000 feet and countless lesser ones without summit access via road that purists can claim for themselves. But there is something inspirational about standing on the highest point around—Katherine Lee Bates was inspired to write "America the Beautiful" while atop Pikes Peak—that shouldn't be denied those who are unable to reach the top without some help. In the case of Pikes Peak, there is a cog railway that ascends the east side that achieves this goal while rendering automobile traffic unnecessary.

onto the roadside or to retrieve our Big Mac at the drive-through. It's a grim picture. But Nature has a way of taking back her own, slowly but surely. Give her enough time—enough for the earth's oil supply to deplete—and she will ultimately restore the balance.

Transportation Problems in Mainstream America

Back on the grid, my conservation track record is spotty in terms of transportation. When I first moved back to

Colorado, I took a job that allowed me to telecommute for the most part. It required only that I go into the office once a week. Unfortunately, the office was one hundred miles to the south in Colorado Springs, and I lived in the Denver area, which automatically put two hundred miles (round trip) on my car each week. On the plus side, my husband, Jason, had the same arrangement, so we carpooled. Still, that was as much as a more local commute would have been.

How Big Is Big Enough?

When I worked in a corporate office, most of my colleagues seemed to adhere to the idea that the car you drove reflected who you were. It turned out to be true. I drove a low-slung Honda CRX, which I nonetheless took off-road to access trailheads so I could climb mountains. Another man drove an equally small Toyota MR2 and used it for the same purpose. The bulk of our coworkers who bought bigger and bigger sport utility vehicles, by contrast, used them for no greater purpose than driving over the speed bumps in the parking lot.

After we got married and had a baby, I quit work and Jason took a job closer to home. Because our consciences still pricked us and gas prices had reached their apex, he took a bus into downtown Denver and left his SUV at home. (Astounding even myself, I had married someone who drove an SUV.) I say it was our conscience, but his motivation had more to do with a lack of affordable parking. Once his company offered him free garage parking, the convenience of driving trumped any good intentions. Such is human behavior, which is why any solution to our collective transportation problem cannot rely on people motivating themselves to do right by the environment.

Then my car died, and Jason changed jobs, with a short hiatus in between. It was a tough year, but at least it motivated us to save money, which meant driving as little as possible. It also meant not replacing my car. Because I hardly drove anywhere anyway, we decided to try being a one-car family to save on a car payment and assuage my guilty conscience. We live in a small town where I can walk most of the places I go on a regular basis, like the grocery store. I pushed the baby in the stroller and sometimes brought the dog on his leash. With no viable bus service to his new job location, my husband took his car to work on a clogged highway for a total round trip commute of nearly two hours, depending on traffic.

> There is no such thing as an environmentally friendly car.

After nine months, we broke down and bought me a car, a used Subaru. Living without a car was, to put it bluntly, a hassle. Eventually it became worth the money to replace my old one, despite the environmental impact.

Then Jason changed jobs again (as I said, it was a tough year, as plenty of Americans can attest), this time to one in Boulder, a forty-five-minute drive to the north. However, bus service became a feasible option again, as did the idea of biking to work—theoretically. It is a long bike ride, some of which is located on the shoulder of a busy highway. A different option would be for Jason to take his bike on the bus until he passed the dangerous part of the route, then ride the rest of the way into work. The downside is that the whole thing would take two hours one way. We are currently considering moving closer to my husband's work now that his job appears more stable.

The point is that in the land of the automobile, we are making a concerted effort—and a big one—to drive as little as possible with the constraints that we must earn a living and public transportation is inadequate or nonexistent. We spend a lot of mental energy considering our transportation options, motivated more by saving money than reducing our ecological footprint. And we drive a lot more than we should but less than other people.

We are just one family who is actually making an effort to conserve, with abysmal results. What of all the other drivers in America who make no effort at all or who feel they have no other option? What is the impact of all our cars on the road? Air pollution, noise pollution, isolation from Nature (overdomestication), lack of exercise and its attending ill health, resources expended to manufacture and power cars. It's enormous.

What is the solution? Own fewer cars and drive them infrequently. Buying an "environmentally friendly" car is a delusion, despite claims to the contrary by the auto companies who want to sell them to you. Between the resources extracted to make it, the energy expended and pollution created to manufacture it, the energy expended and pollution created to ship it to a dealer, and the environmental cost to drive it and ultimately dispose of it, there is no such thing as an environmentally friendly car.

*In the meantime, until we find a
good solution, the best alternative is
to use less by driving less, not simply
replacing cars with "greener" cars.*

If I *were* to imagine an eco-friendly car, though, it would look like this. It would be built from 100 percent recycled metal, recycled plastic, and recycled tires. The engine could be diesel running on biodiesel fuel or 100 percent vegetable oil. Or it could run on synthetic natural gas made from biomass. It could even be electric, if the electricity that ran it were sustainably produced, which would be difficult to verify until all electricity is sustainably produced. The car would be small and basic to keep its raw materials to a minimum. And it would be built to last for decades.

It's not so far-fetched. Researchers are currently working on ways to convert biomass into low-carbon transportation fuels. A recent Nature Conservancy study concluded that the best sources of plant material for biomass fuels were food waste, damaged trees, algae, and corn stover. The reason these win out is that they don't require land that could otherwise be used productively to be converted to a crop cultivated specifically to become fuel.

Biodiesel created from algae, including saltwater algae, could be commercially viable as early as 2012, according to the April 2009 issue of *Biodiesel Magazine*, although it won't hit the mainstream until somewhat later.

The research is promising, but any solution driven by technology will come with a set of unintended consequences. We must be careful to develop them in concert with Nature so we don't wind up messing things up further. Take, for example, the idea of biodiesel created from algae. Where will we get the algae? How much do we need? More than occurs naturally? Can we overharvest it to ill consequence? If we grow our own, how will that change the ecosystem? Before we devote ourselves to any new solution, we had better think it through carefully so we don't create a new and different adverse impact upon the earth. It's conscious decision-making on a commercial rather than a personal scale.[49]

In the meantime, until we find a good solution, the best alternative is to use less by driving less, not simply replacing cars with "greener" cars. Use less of the earth's raw materials, energy, and fossil fuels. Create less waste and pollution by using less. This is a tall order, since the American car culture is firmly entrenched. We need a huge shift in attitude away from self-entitlement and toward good stewardship of the earth through collective effort. We can all do our part.

There are two main problems in America that hinder us from driving less: one of infrastructure and one of attitude—or motivation, depending on how you look at it. We currently have no incentive to tackle environmental issues caused by our preferred mode of transportation, unless we can steel ourselves to short-term sacrifice for long-term gain. No motivation except acting in good conscience, and even then the lack of infrastructure can be frustrating.

I once worked with an idealistic colleague in Colorado Springs who wanted to take the bus to work because of his deep commitment to environmental stewardship. In the pre-Internet days, he tried in vain to locate a

World War II Gas Rationing

Two short generations ago, this country knew how to conserve. We did it because we were all working toward a common goal: winning the Second World War. Everything from sugar and coffee to typewriters and bicycles was rationed so that the nation's resources could be devoted to the troops. Citizens on the home front willingly and enthusiastically did their part—except, that is, for gasoline. The government first called for voluntary gas rationing. But as this proved to be ineffective, by 1942 the Office of Price Administration took over and issued ration coupon books to force people to comply. Everyone but truck drivers (who carried goods around the country) had to limit their driving. Rationing ended several months after the war did in 1945, and the American love affair with the automobile revved up again.

current route map and schedule by calling the main bus terminal, the city office, and even checking out the posters at bus stops. There was no direct route from where he lived to where he worked (since the city grew with no thought to nonautomobile transportation), and he couldn't get anyone to tell him how to connect. One day he simply tried it and asked the bus driver. His first bus dropped him off at a stop on one side of a busy thoroughfare (with no marked crosswalk), and his connecting bus arrived to pick him up two minutes later on the other side. My colleague had to dash across the road and pray for perfect split-second timing among the traffic to make his connection. If he missed it, he would have had to wait another forty-five minutes for the next bus. Going home was no better. Eventually, despite his commitment, he gave up in disgust.

My colleague had the option of driving a car instead, even if he didn't like it. As altruistic as his motivation was, it wasn't enough to alter his consumer behavior in the face of too much hassle. The carrot never works as well as the stick in cases where the consequences of a person's actions are felt only by someone else, in this case future generations and the health of the planet.

The carrot never works as well as the stick in cases where the consequences of a person's actions are felt only by someone else, in this case future generations and the health of the planet.

But when the consequences are felt by the person taking action, people are capable of extraordinary feats. I have another friend in Denver whose car lease ended in the middle of winter, and she couldn't afford to renew it or buy another car. Her night shift job was a forty-minute drive from her house, and her low hourly wage meant she couldn't afford to quit. Her motivation was the fear of not being able to pay her rent or meet her bills, rather than that of my colleague, who was simply trying to do the right thing. My friend in Denver very quickly located the bus schedule and discovered that the closest stop was over a mile away. So she jury-rigged her old bicycle and rode it to and from the bus stop in the dark and the cold and the snow to make it to work on time. She did this for the remainder of the winter until she was able to buy a used car. Without making it her explicit goal, she reduced her ecological footprint because no other options were financially feasible.

Creative Solutions

What needs to be done to motivate the average American to take public transportation? To move away from our car-centric attitude? To walk, ride a bike, or even carpool to work? What must happen to motivate people to vote for the infrastructure (i.e., functioning, practical bus and/ or train systems; bike lanes; pedestrian paths) in the first place? A spike in gas prices would help and is inevitably headed in our direction, but we have a lot to overcome.

A truly creative solution is one that addresses multiple problems at once. I have an idea for a city like Colorado Springs that would address traffic and all its attendant problems (pollution, congestion, accidents, road rage), plus recreation, public health, animal habitats, and economic development. It's quite simple: connect all parks and open spaces in the city by bike and pedestrian paths.

Colorado Springs is a city of beautiful natural scenery situated at the foot of Pikes Peak along Colorado's Front Range where the plains meet the mountains. Like most cities in the American West with plenty of land, Colorado Springs turned this asset into a liability by letting the city sprawl unchecked onto the eastern plains and by thinking only in terms of driving when planning for transportation infrastructure.

However, the typical Colorado Springs resident enjoys spending time outdoors, and the city is filled with parks and other open spaces such as designated fields and forests that cannot be developed. Each one has its own microecosystem and is populated by the types of animals normally found in urban and suburban centers—song-birds, birds of prey, squirrels, rabbits, foxes, and coyotes—as well as deer, bear, and the occasional mountain lion (it is still the Wild West in a sense, after all).

Colorado Springs is also home to the Olympic Training Center and USA Cycling, a healthy community of road and mountain bikers and a thriving group of tri-athletes. In other words, people like to ride bikes in this town. As such, you would expect there to be bike paths all over. But there aren't.

When I lived and worked there, I considered bik-ing to work for health and environmental reasons, but I found the idea daunting because of my preconceived notion of biking to work as the domain of the triathlon and bike racer crowd. They had expensive bikes and shiny spandex outfits, plus fancy bags to hold their laptops and work clothes. They commuted on shoulders of congested roads with no real bike lanes and in all kinds of weather and had the confidence to brave the traffic. They were, in short, intimidating. So I never biked to work.

But it doesn't have to look like that. I have a friend who lives in Munich, which is a bike- and pedestrian-friendly city because the order-loving Germans take non-car transportation quite seriously. Munich's bike lanes are on sidewalks the width of a typical American street. Each sidewalk on major streets has a bike lane and a separate pedestrian lane, and bikers are expected to ride in the direction of traffic. In other words, each sidewalk has bikes going in only one direction. You can get a ticket if you violate this law. Or, as my friend found out, you can be smacked on the head by a law-abiding vigilante who is going the correct direction.

Thousands of Munich's residents bike to work in safety. When they arrive, they find long stands of bike racks to which they can lock their bikes. No one wears spandex. My friend's wife biked to work daily, even at eight months pregnant, when I met her. She wore work clothes and sensible shoes and carried her regular bag slung over one shoulder. She also rode slowly on a large, sturdy bike with big tires. She wasn't trying to get a work-out, look cool, or impress anyone. She simply needed to get to work in an efficient, inexpensive manner. The lay-out of the city and its non-car-centric culture made that possible in a way that it wasn't in Colorado Springs.

It is frustrating that a city like Colorado Springs—with residents who like to bike, a climate that allows for it with three hundred sunny days per year, and plenty of existing open space—cannot find the funds or political wherewithal to see the solution that is staring them in the face. If they would simply connect all the parks and open spaces to each other via a paved path, then even ordinary nontriathletes like me could take advantage of them. If the average person had an easy way to bike to work without having to dodge cars, it would lighten the traffic on the roads. The obvious benefits would include less congestion, less pollution, less frequent road mainte-nance, and fewer accidents. On a personal level, anyone who biked—or, for that matter, walked—to work even once a week would reap the health benefits of regular exercise outside in the fresh air and sunshine. They would also save money on gas and wear and tear on their automobiles, not to mention doctor visits and gym memberships.

The ease of getting to and from parks would also increase outdoor recreation. Promoting such a healthful lifestyle would make the city an appealing place to live, which in turn would attract companies that wanted to take advantage of a stable workforce. (And a healthy one, which still matters since our corporations continue to largely foot the bill for health insurance in this country.)

A more subtle benefit would be for the environment itself. If the paths were lined with trees and bushes, or skirted the open spaces, they would create greenways for the birds and small mammals to expand their habitats. Cities and especially suburbs are known for paving over natural habitats, naming streets after the trees they have cut down. This idea could reverse that trend. Win-win-win.

It is difficult to tell if we are close to snatching victory from the jaws of defeat, as ideas like this one could, or snatching defeat from the jaws of victory. Unless we overcome the infrastructure problems and the entrenched mindsets, the latter could very well happen. In fact, unless we ditch the mindsets, we will never overcome the infrastructure issues that require money and voter approval.

The mindsets are not just car-centric, but even more deeply rooted than that. Our country was founded on the principles of the rights of individuals, which has led to the idea that each individual should be independent. To state it slightly differently, if you are independent, you are not dependent on anyone else; therefore, you need to own your own car.

But what is wrong with being interdependent? What about sharing? Carpools are a form of sharing.[50] So is taking a taxi, and if you rarely drive, it may even save you money to get rid of your car and only take cabs. Using public transportation constitutes sharing. When I traveled to Europe, I was able to take public transportation within and between every city I wanted to visit. But if you come to America, you can't do the same. You are thwarted by our car-centric attitude. For example, you can't take a train going north or south in this country unless you live on the coasts.

B-cycle

Bike-share programs are cropping up in the United States. Denver has a program through a company called B-cycle. Bike stands (called B-stations) exist throughout the city, clustered in the downtown area, and bikes are easy-to-ride cruisers with baskets on the handlebars. You can pay daily or become a member if you plan on using the bikes frequently. Simply locate a B-station, select a bike, pay with a credit card at the kiosk (or enter your membership information), then ride it as long as you like. When you are finished, return it to the closest B-station. B-cycle plans to expand its business across the United States in the near future.[51]

Any idea that involves using a collectively owned mode of transportation is a form of sharing and lessens our impact on the earth. There are bike-share and car-share programs in cities all over the globe. They make financial sense too, especially if you live in a city where owning a car comes with a price tag of more than just the car payment. Exorbitant parking garage fees (or the hassle of finding elusive on-street parking) and high insurance rates add up. Don't own a car or even a bike; instead join a program to share one owned by somebody else.

Zipcar

For people whose needs (or desires) require a car instead of a bike, there are car-share programs. The largest car-share program in the world, Zipcar, was started in America and has expanded to Canada and the U.K., with plans to continue expansion across Europe. It operates similarly to bike-share programs, except that you get a car instead. Simply become a member, reserve a car, unlock it using your membership card, and start driving. They offer two different membership plans: the Occasional Driving Plan for pay-as-you-go members and Extra Value Plans for people who are using ZipCars as their primary mode of transportation. As a bonus, if you are a ZipCar member in any city, you can drive a ZipCar in any other city, which is cheaper than renting a car.[52]

Our biggest problem is one of attitude, and it had been getting worse from the turn of the new millennium until the financial and housing market crashes put the brakes on unrestrained spending. I'm hoping the new frugality will spark a change in attitude toward driving habits. A colleague of mine once declared he couldn't drive his children in anything other than an SUV because they needed the space. With an altered attitude, he may now realize that plenty of other options exist.

He can pack three of them in the backseat of a Buick Regal like my parents did with my two sisters and me. Yes, we wore seat belts, and no, we didn't have a TV to entertain us. We had to entertain ourselves or sit and be bored, which wasn't a death sentence. (It built character, or so we were told.) Sometimes we argued, particularly over who had to sit in the middle. Nobody was scarred for life.

He can make his kids ride their bikes if their destination isn't too far. They can all fit nicely on a bus or a train together. Or they can lighten their schedules, stop driving all over town, and instead stay home and do something together as a family.

That's what I mean about creative solutions. That's what it means to use less. It means getting over your sense of entitlement and asking whether the planet can truly afford your actions. It means voting for public transportation projects that come along for the future. (Or actively lobbying for them.) And it means using your car less in the meantime in whatever way you see fit. It means stopping to smell the roses that can thrive in pollution-free air.

☞ 8 ☜

Stuff

Possession isn't nine-tenths of the law. It's nine-tenths of the problem.

—John Lennon

B EFORE MOVING TO TAOS, I owned a townhouse in Colorado Springs that was almost two thousand square feet and had a two-car garage, plus lots of closet space, all of it full. I remember walking through the place before I bought it and thinking to myself how conscientious the builder had been to include so much storage space. I was at a point in my life when I was tired of moving around and just wanted to put down some roots, unpack everything I owned in one spot, and throw away the boxes. Copious storage space was a factor in my decision to buy that particular townhouse.

It seems to be a selling point in general in America: "Oversized garage!" "Tons of storage space!" But when you think about it, what does ample storage space imply?

What does it say about our values that we own so much stuff that we can't use it all at once? My whole townhouse was filled with the stuff accumulated after a decade or so in the working world. Even as I got rid of the stuff I didn't need, I replaced it with more stuff. After I built my house in Taos and had enough stuff to fill it from the stuff in my townhouse without buying anything additional, I figured I had reached my limit. How much stuff does one person need, after all?

With that realization, long before I moved, I decided to clean out my garage. It took sustained effort over two weekends, but I succeeded in emptying it except for the most important stuff: my car, my skis, and my snow tires. Then I turned my attention to the closets. Thinning them out turned out to be easy, despite my clothes' propensity to breed. I disliked my work wardrobe and had vowed never to wear uncomfortable clothing, such as pantyhose, heels, or suits again. Some things are just not necessary in my life.

As for the rest of the stuff I had stuffed into every crevice, my theory was that if I hadn't used it in the past two years, I didn't need it. I carted one carload after another to Goodwill and donated perfectly good items that other people would put to better use than I had been.[53]

Once I started ridding my living space of extraneous possessions, I realized two things. First, my living space was too big. And second, the rest of my life could use a little housecleaning as well. After more than ten years in an industry that made me increasingly uncomfortable (defense contracting), I looked around me and realized that I had less and less in common with my colleagues every year. I didn't aspire to wealth, power, or recognition. I wasn't out to impress anyone with my possessions, social status, or looks. I didn't want to drive a big, gas-guzzling car. What that meant was that I had less and less I could share with the people surrounding me for eight hours (or more) a day. That was a drag. It really was. It was a drag on my soul as well as my conscience.

As I uncluttered my house and wrestled with my conscience, I also plotted my escape. The best (possibly the only) things I got out of my corporate job were a good salary and benefits. The deal was that I would give them my time, energy, and skills, and they would give me money. The fine print that I had only skimmed said that I would also give them my ideals, principles, physical fitness, and mental stability. In exchange, they would give me stress, "core values," and lip service to work-life balance—ironically, a phrase coined by the corporate world where there is none.

The downside to me was obvious once I stepped back and looked at it: I was sacrificing all aspects of a healthful life for a paycheck. To compound it, I was immersed in a culture that exerted pressure to spend that paycheck on stuff I didn't need or even really want. And I was placing an enormous strain on the earth's natural resources.

From a corporate perspective, the disadvantage is that once workers figure out the exchange and decide they want more time and less stress, they decide that forfeiting the money is an option. I wanted the time. So I quit my job, sold my townhouse, and moved to my spartan paradise in the high desert.

Sometimes I strike a self-righteous tone when I tell people that I lived without a TV, computer, or any of the electronic equipment that has come to dominate our indoor landscapes. But what it really boiled down to initially was that I simply didn't have room in my

688-square-foot house to fit it all in. That's why I gave them away. I'm not against TV or the Internet. But after having lived without them, I know they are not necessary for a healthful, satisfying life.

I will go even further and declare that I learned they are bad for you, although not in the ways that most of us believe (e.g., excessive screen time ruining your eyes or too much time on the couch undermining your health). It was something else that I hadn't even considered in my sanctimonious anti-TV preaching.

In my Taos cloister, I was removed from the daily blitzkrieg of ads on TV, radio, magazines, billboards, newspapers, and the Internet, none of which I encountered on a regular basis. I had lived there full-time for only a month when it occurred to me that certain pressures I had taken for granted as being internal were actually societally imposed and had evaporated. Because I never watched TV, no longer spent hours every day online, quit reading celebrity magazines, and wasn't exposed to advertisements, I had ceased to care about what I wore, what trends I was missing, and whether people liked me. I had total freedom to simply be myself.

The best part was that it felt completely normal. In my previous existence, I would have looked at such a person as being eccentric. Those types of people weren't current on the hottest infotainment dustup, didn't have the urge to jump on the latest bandwagon (or rail against it), and didn't envy the lifestyles of the rich and famous. Secretly, I envied them. By the time I got to Taos, I had my own eccentricities ("normal" people don't build off-grid straw bale houses) and had resigned myself to being thought of as unconventional. But in Taos, I realized that the feelings of eccentricity had stemmed from the social pressure, however inadvertent, of having mainstream people around. It was amazing how quickly that pressure lifted once I left "civilized" society.

Now that I am back in the mainstream in Colorado, I am subject again to the bombardment. We are all assaulted by near-constant ads, and they exert an enormous psychological pressure on us to buy stuff we don't need. Yet having been away from it for so long, I find I react differently than I had before my time off the grid.

We are all assaulted by near-constant ads, and they exert an enormous psychological pressure on us to buy stuff we don't need.

Instead of feeling social pressure to buy useless stuff, I feel annoyed that someone is trying to influence me to reclutter my life. I disregard ads for items that serve no purpose in my life: trendy junk to strew around . . . I mean, to decorate my house. Electronic widgets that were wholly unnecessary to me in Taos. New maternity and postbaby clothes when barely worn hand-me-downs will suffice.

This is not to say I don't buy stuff. Living frugally doesn't have to mean depriving yourself. Rather, it means making the same kinds of conscious decisions for your bank account that you do for the environment. I buy what I need, using my off-grid definition of *need*. I also indulge my weakness for books, which are the sole objects I allow to clutter most horizontal surfaces in our house. But I do limit my trips to bookstores because I can easily spend fifty dollars within half an hour. Apart from that, I rarely shop.

Not shopping is a terrific strategy for using less, as well as spending less money. It saves you from making the kind of impulse purchases that wind up cluttering your closets or garage. Shopping only for necessities, plus the few extras that are on top of your list of niceties, ensures you consume as little as possible but without it feeling like a sacrifice. Because you decide what extras you are willing to buy (such as books in my case), you keep the pleasures that are important to you in your life. And the reduced exposure to the lure of impulse purchases immediately lightens your burden of debt and clutter without causing any pain.

Do You Need It? Can You Afford It? Where Will You Put It?

Toward the end of my year off the grid, I went to a craft fair with a friend. Taos regularly hosts these kinds of events throughout the summer and fall. Artists and artisans across the spectrum set up booths to sell their work. Some of it is kitschy, and some is beautiful. It's all in the eye of the beholder.

After having spent nearly a year buying nothing but essentials, I found every object desirable: hand-blown glassware, Nature photographs, hand-dipped candles, funky jewelry, objets d'art made from household items, hand-painted throw pillows, raku pottery, hand-crocheted scarves. I lusted after them all. I made mental notes of which booths I wanted to revisit once I had narrowed down what I wanted to buy to two or three things. My friend bought a CD of Native American flute music; I almost bought a Native American flute, which I don't know how to play. I considered buying sage smudge sticks, which are bundles of sagebrush that can be lighted with a match so they burn slowly and give off an incense-like scent, even though I could easily have harvested the sage outside my own door to make my own or filled my house with the heady aroma simply by opening my windows.

I felt as if I had been starving without even knowing it and then had stumbled upon a feast. I didn't know where to begin. The urge to open my wallet and start handing over money was strong, so strong that it surprised me. So I asked myself three questions as I evaluated each item I wanted to buy. Do I need it? Can I afford it? Where will I put it?

I didn't need any of them, but I didn't want that to preclude my buying a small trinket that would give me pleasure. Living on savings, I couldn't justify buying anything over twenty-five dollars, although that still left plenty of choices. A small packet of note cards with Nature photographs was only fifteen dollars, or I could have gotten a set of candles or even the CD of flute music.

It was the third question that limited me the most. Living in a small house that was already full of stuff, I had no room for new stuff. My bookshelves and windowsills were full, as was every other useful flat surface. There was room on the walls for pictures, but I already had a box of them under the bed that I was too timid to hang. Some of my interior walls are frame walls, and they are full. The exterior walls are all straw bale, which requires special hardware to hang pictures (especially heavy ones). I didn't have the guts to try it because I was worried I would mess it up. When I finally work up the courage, I have the contents of that box waiting to be displayed.

In the end, I bought nothing. My small house had saved me from spending money unnecessarily. A few days after the craft fair, I could hardly recall a single thing that I couldn't live without. It had been enough to saturate my senses by simply walking around admiring everything. I have the memory of the experience to sustain me, no purchase required.

Those questions moved back on the grid with me and currently help to keep my spending in check and the clutter at bay, even with a baby. They are the opposite of shopping as a hobby, "retail therapy," or making purchases out of convenience. But it's harder back in the mainstream since I have plugged back into TV and the Internet with their attendant onslaught of advertising.

In my tiny on-grid house, I still mostly don't buy stuff I don't need because we lack the space to house it. The list of things I don't buy at the grocery store includes frozen food, desserts, most processed foods, junk food, prepackaged snack food, soda, most condiments, household cleaning products, anything with a chemical scent added, hair care products apart from shampoo and conditioner, products touted as disposable, and pretty much anything that is manufactured and packaged by a corporation that I can easily make myself (such as glass cleaner: white vinegar and water) or do without (such as dryer sheets, which I haven't used since college). Our refrigerator is small and our cabinet space limited. So we do without and don't really notice.

If you are looking for a way to spend less (and therefore use less), try declaring a "material fast."

If you are looking for a way to spend less (and therefore use less), try declaring a "material fast." Spend no money for one month except on your fixed bills. Take your credit cards out of your wallet and put in a twenty-dollar bill. Forcing yourself to pay cash for daily sundries will quickly disabuse you of the idea that you don't know where your money goes. You probably do know, but you are turning a blind eye. It will also highlight your priorities. If you have to lay that twenty down on the counter to buy a doughnut and a coffee and only sixteen and change remain, you might rethink the junk food. You might bring a sack lunch of leftovers to work and decline the invitations to go out to eat. You might read the tabloid headlines at the newsstand where you are buying a pack of gum but resist the urge to buy the magazine, and possibly the gum.

For an interesting experiment, keep track of each purchase you don't make and see how much you don't spend. Did you really need the magazine? The doughnut? The widget that always appeals to you that you already own twelve of? If you are truly ambitious, you could write yourself a check for the total amount and put it in your savings account. And if that makes you smile, do it again next month. Next thing you know, you will have enough to fully fund an IRA.

But that's not all. Make note too of how spending less provides psychological as well as financial relief. If you are in debt, lessening the amount you continue to rack up will lift a burden from your shoulders. If you have been unable to save for a rainy day, you will be pleasantly surprised to have some extra cash at the end of the month.

The most subtle benefit of all is for the planet. The less we all buy, the less is produced to meet the reduced demand. That translates to fewer of the earth's resources being expended to support a habit of buying unnecessary items, which add pounds to your hips or prevent you from building up a financial cushion for the future.

These days I am less connected to the land than I was in Taos and more connected with the manmade world, and that makes me feel uneasy. But every time I choose not to buy a cheap plastic baby toy and I ask myself those three questions, I remind myself that I am doing a favor for the earth as well as my bank account. It is more satisfying than adding to the clutter.

Consumers, Conservers, and Citizens

It may sound tedious to think through all of your decisions in such depth. Isn't it easier just to plunk down a credit card and buy your way out of a problem? Perhaps. But there are costs associated with this kind of solution that go far beyond your own pocketbook.

If you watch enough news, you will hear the word *consumer* bandied about importantly. "The Consumer Price Index is up." "Consumer confidence is down." "Consumers spent less during this holiday season than the one last year." You can read consumer reports and feel secure that consumer protection rights are overseen by consumer advocates. You can find headlines everywhere having to do with consumer prices, consumer demand, consumer sentiment, consumer goods, and, of course, consumer spending.

Amid all the attention lavished on the consumer, it would be easy to think of ourselves solely in these terms. Indeed, that is how we seem to have characterized ourselves over the past two decades of unchecked consumption. During the technology boom at the end of the last century, we consumed more and more stuff right up until the day the bubble burst and startled us back to our senses. In debt, laid off, or simply worn out, we the consumers could no longer consume, and the country slipped into a short recession.

Too short, in hindsight. Not long enough for us to learn a lesson. Just when we thought the Internet boom of the '90s had been distinguished by overconsumption, along came the housing bubble in the new millennium to show us we were capable of consuming even more.

Flashy lifestyles became the norm. The term *conspicuous consumption* was no longer an insult. And, with cheap credit accessible to virtually everybody, anyone with a materialistic dream could find the cash to fulfill it.

At the same time, environmentalism went mainstream and even had a kind of cachet in certain circles. "Green" was the new black, and everyone wanted a piece of it. In America's market-driven economy, advertisers could repackage their products with "green" labels and persuade us to part with our dollars to save the environment. The goal was to get us to keep buying, and the method was to convince us that we wanted—or rather, *needed*—more stuff, but this time it was eco-friendly stuff that the earth allegedly needed us to need too. Environmentalism was simply another piece of bait in the feeding frenzy.

If anyone had stopped to ask why we all needed bigger, better, faster, newer, greener, or simply more stuff, it never made it into mainstream media because that kind of talk didn't sell ads. When the party ended in the crash of 2008, millions of us were left with the nastiest sort of hangover: more debt than we could handle, a precarious job market, and the possibility of losing our houses along with the stuff inside them. All of a sudden, the idea of living a quiet, affordable life, with a decent job, surrounded by family and friends instead of possessions, seemed much more appealing. Instead of having to acquire more, it became OK to be satisfied with having just enough. It was time to stop being labeled a consumer—one who consumes—and find a new label. I'd like to suggest conserver: one who conserves. Or citizen: an inhabitant of a place.

An Invitation to Dinner

Everyone wants an invitation to my Aunt Jan and Uncle Alan's house for dinner. The live in a '70s-era townhome that they have never updated. It lacks a formal dining room, gourmet kitchen, walk-in wine cellar, and even a main-level guest bathroom. (You have to go upstairs.) Aunt Jan has a thermometer inside her oven because she doesn't trust its temperature gauge to be accurate. Uncle Alan keeps their wine collection in sawed-off PVC pipes in an overhead cabinet. But they throw the most sought-after dinner parties around. The reason? They are gracious hosts. Aunt Jan is an excellent cook, and Uncle Alan knows his way around drinkable (and affordable) table wine. They come from the era when hosting a party meant inviting the right mix of people to ensure lively conversation. Aunt Jan knows how to make her guests feel comfortable and interesting (the key: she knows how to listen), and Uncle Alan keeps the conversation moving with a well-timed joke. They are not out to impress. They are simply interested in people of all ages and personalities, and it shows.

If you inhabit planet earth, it is in your best interests to *conserve* its resources, which the Oxford English Dictionary defines as protecting them "from harm, destruction, or wasteful overuse." When the resources are gone, they're gone. All the money in the world won't bring them back.

The Siege of Leningrad

The Siege of Leningrad during World War II offers a chilling analogy to today's environmental predicament. The siege lasted seventeen months, during which 1.2 million people died. Starving or freezing to death were the most common fates, and food and fuel the scarcest commodities. As such, the market should, by conventional thinking, have set their prices accordingly high. It did for a while. But the problem was that when the food ran out, it didn't matter how much money you had left: you still starved. The better decision was to conserve the food supply and to ration it until such time as more could be obtained. Conservation trumped consumption.

Our energy supplies and other planetary resources are dwindling ever more rapidly as the earth's human population grows. The world with its nearly seven billion people could very well run out of fossil fuel–supplied energy before we can produce enough from renewable sources to satiate our current and projected rates of consumption. We should be conserving, not consuming, energy. Rationing, not guzzling it. When the world's oil runs out, it doesn't matter how much money you earn, you still won't be able to drive that SUV. The same goes for our essential resources such as food and water and others such as trees, minerals, or even raw land.

The planet already has a large-enough population to support using finite resources, and it's getting even larger. If we continue our current patterns of "harm, destruction, and wasteful overuse," we will one day run out of the resources that support our way of life, and that day may come sooner than we expect. This is a preventable catastrophe, if we start now and act wisely. Are you doing your part to help out? Do your actions matter in the long run? What can one small person out of seven billion do to make a difference anyway?

Use less and spend less: it's the essence of conservation. Depending on your motivation, you can use less and therefore spend less, or you can spend less and therefore use less, whichever suits you. It works both ways. When you make purchasing decisions according to conservation- or thrift-minded values rather than according to society's values, conservation and thrift become an intrinsic part of your life and no longer feel like a sacrifice. The benefits are legion.

Consume means "use up," "do away with completely," and "spend wastefully." Synonyms include *squander* and *destroy*. It is no coincidence that while we have been squandering our money, we have been destroying the environment. Buying material goods—the stuff that clutters our homes and our lives—is a cause of both.

Now, after two long bull runs of unrestrained consumption, it is time to conserve. The simplest way to accomplish this is to use less.

Use less what? Use less gas in your car, heat in your house, food on your table, and stuff in general. While you're at it, spend less money, experience less stress, and feel more satisfied with the way you live your life.

I keep using the word *stuff* because it doesn't actually matter what the stuff is. Everybody has the item they can't get enough of. For me, it's books. I feel compelled to own the books I read, and I rarely give them away after I have read them. The shelves on my bookcases in Taos each have two neat rows of books, one behind the other, and any books that don't fit have migrated to my nightstand, dresser, and one lucky windowsill. For a friend of mine, it's coats. She clearly and painfully remembers not being able to afford a winter coat in high school, and she has spent more than necessary to overcompensate with a closet full of them in her adult life. What is it for you? Clothes? Shoes? Electronics? Jewelry? A new car every two years? Home remodeling? Garden tools? Sports equipment?

Owning more stuff will not make you happier, as has been lately experienced by large segments of our population. Yet until recently we all continued to buy and use more stuff. But to what end? I can't figure it out. To impress each other? To convince ourselves that we are worthwhile human beings? Is it simply addictive? Using more means spending more money: do you have the money to spend?

The impact goes beyond your own pocketbook. Using more also means using more of the planet's resources. Every item you buy has an associated cost to the earth that isn't fully reflected in its price tag. It includes the raw materials that must be extracted from the earth to make the item, the energy used in its manufacture, the pollution and waste by-products created during its production, and the pollution created and energy expended during its transportation from the factory to your home.

The more stuff we all buy, the higher that cost is to the earth. It manifests itself as global warming, deforestation, animal habitat destruction, holes in the ozone layer, dead zones where rivers meet the ocean, plummeting fish stocks, melting glaciers, acid rain, polluted groundwater, and uncontrollable smog. Excess consumption in America is one of the primary drivers of the earth's environmental woes. Especially as economies have gone global and the stuff we consume comes from the four corners of the planet, Americans' patterns of overconsumption have further-reaching effects than they ever did.

This equally applies to products that are touted as being environmentally friendly. They may use recycled materials for their manufacture instead of newly extracted raw ones. They might be produced using less energy and creating less pollution than a traditional manufacturing process. They still must be transported from the site of manufacture to your home. These products are typically thought of as being environmentally friendly because of the way they are used (such as "green" household cleaning products), but they still have an environmental cost associated with them.

And the answer is still the same: use less of them. It makes no sense to replace the polyester sheets on your bed with organic cotton ones until the ones you already own wear out. It's ridiculous to rip out the existing floor in your kitchen and install a new bamboo one unless the original floor is unsafe, worn out, or irreparably damaged. It is wholly unnecessary to buy a "green" window cleaner that comes in a plastic bottle when white vinegar and water will do. There is no point in buying natural detergent if you use three times as much of it than your clothes require.

Environmental Costs

Even "green" products such as compact fluorescent light bulbs have an environmental cost. A CFL bulb is composed of glass (which may or may not include recycled glass as a raw material), plastic (a petroleum product), metal (especially if they use electronic ballasts that contain printed circuit boards), and a gas (typically mercury vapor). The CFL bulb must be manufactured, which uses energy and causes pollution, and transported to retail stores and end users, which does the same. At the end of its useful life, it must be disposed of properly because mercury is poisonous even at the small amount contained in it. (CFL supporters can make the argument that using CFLs instead of incandescent bulbs actually reduces mercury emissions because mercury is released when coal is burned to supply the extra electricity incandescent bulbs use. I call this hairsplitting. Turn your lights off when you don't need them and buy fewer light bulbs overall.)

In all of these cases, using less to begin with, putting off a purchase until the need becomes crucial, or making do with something you already own will save you money as well.

Necessities versus Niceties

The root of the problem is that we have been conditioned to consume. Shopping is an American pastime.

Advertisers have become so adept at convincing us we need their products that we no longer question them.

They prey on your fears. *Your home is not safe without one.* (Even though we lived safely without it for centuries.)

They play on your insecurities. *Everybody else has one.* (You won't measure up without it.)

They appeal to your ego. *You have enough money to buy one, and you are important enough to own one.* (Even if you don't really need one.)

Relentless advertising coupled with improved standards of living have conspired to render us unable to distinguish between necessities and niceties.

Relentless advertising coupled with improved standards of living have conspired to render us unable to distinguish between necessities and niceties. A necessity is something required to sustain human life. Very few things are necessities: healthful food, simple but comfortable shelter, clean water, renewable energy, and sociable companionship. That's really about it, and that's all I had living off the grid in Taos. Clothes are a necessity, but can easily stray into the nicety category. Olive once sold all her clothes at a yard sale except for two black dresses. She lived happily for a while, free from the bondage of fashion, until slowly color crept back in and her wardrobe expanded again. Once I quit work, I gave away half my wardrobe and didn't bother to replace it even when I reentered the corporate world.

Frugal Sports Gear

I learned my first lesson in frugal sports gear from my friend Ann P. I once persuaded her to do a five-kilometer snowshoe race for charity, using the argument that it was all downhill and could therefore be fun instead of competitive. Ann drove, and we stopped for tea along the way. I climbed out of the passenger seat and opened the back door to pull my purse out of my backpack. In doing so, I inadvertently pulled my ski pants out too and dropped them on the ground. My two-hundred-dollar, Gore-Tex, breathable, windproof, waterproof, ripstop, name-brand pants. I didn't notice they were gone until we got to the race miles down the road. Then I freaked out, ransacking Ann's car.

"It's only money," she told me.

She was right, of course, but my frugal streak runs pretty deep, and I felt like I had dropped two hundred dollars cash down a storm drain. The day turned out to be warm, so I did the race in my sweatpants. No big deal.

Later, I went to a ski shop and asked for their cheapest pants as replacement. They had a thin pair of no-name pants for thirty dollars. But, as the salesman warned me knowledgeably, "They don't breathe," as if it were of primary concern to such an obviously hardcore mountaineer as myself. That was over ten years ago, and I haven't cared yet. These pants have seen so much use that they have duct tape on the rear from where I glissaded down a snow slope and over some rocks and tore them. I still don't care, nor have I replaced them. That was my gear turning point, and it influenced the way I looked at consumer purchases in the rest of my life.

Think hard about what constitutes a necessity in your life, and be honest in your answers. You'll know if you are lying to yourself. Manufactured products, for the most part, are not necessary. If it didn't exist one hundred years ago, it is not a necessity. Among the items that are not truly necessities are the ones I lacked at my house in Taos: refrigerator, dishwasher, clothes washer/dryer, microwave, computer, TV, and central heating among them. These are called niceties or conveniences, and if you let them, they will take over your life and your bank account.

Do You Really Need It?

We tend to overuse the word *need*. I had a conversation early on with my mother about growing a garden in front of my house in Taos.

"You need a garden hose," she said.

"Technically, I don't need a hose," I answered. "I have a watering can that I can fill from the spigot."

"But you will have to make too many trips back and forth," she replied.

"I don't mind," I said. "I will use less water and get some exercise that way."

She gave me a hose anyway, and I wound up never using it because I was too concerned about conserving water. It lay scorching in the sun for years, eventually drying up to the point where it cracked and became unusable as a hose. But it's still there in front of my house in case I can think of something else to do with it.

This is not to say that we shouldn't own some niceties. Quitting materialism cold turkey is too difficult for most us, including me. I lived a nonmaterialistic life for one year before moving back on-grid and resuming some (but not nearly all) of my former consumption habits. I decided that as long as I bought material goods sparingly and with full knowledge that they are not required to live a satisfying life, then making an impact on the earth's environment with some convenience purchases was alright. I still use less than the average American.

But why do we want to own excessive amounts of stuff to begin with? Living off the grid and out of touch (and on savings) for a year broke me of that desire. I managed to fill my space and time differently and discovered I was vastly more satisfied with my life and myself than I had been before.

In Taos, since I had the time, I chose to start reconnecting with my long-neglected spiritual side. Going to meditation and dharma talks on a weekly basis helped, as did spending more time outside wondering at the mystery of creation all around me. I read a lot too, absorbing ideas of faith and different belief systems from the books I selected.

But there was something else that allowed me to open up to spirituality, and it surprised me to recognize that it was giving away the bulk of my possessions to scale down for my small house. Once I let go of possessing and acquiring, I was free from feeling the need to possess and acquire. Stuff, after all, is just stuff. The only reason I had acquired so much in the first place was from a societally imposed pressure to keep up with the Joneses. Keeping up with the Joneses seems to have evolved recently into a national pastime of outdoing the Joneses. Everyone seems to want to live the way only rich people used to twenty years ago. Everyone feels the need to own luxury items they can't afford. When did we all decide we needed granite countertops? If the neighbors have them, we want them too.

The Spiritual Consequence of Clutter

I live in a neighborhood where many of the residents have storage sheds. I am surprised at how frequently a new shed pops up on another lot. I can't help but think that we are a culture that cherishes our stuff so much we keep it forever. We seem to think that the one who has the most stuff has won some sort of prize, even if it is only the envy of our neighbors. We fill our homes with stuff and then build a shed, and then rent a storage unit, and finally put a PODS storage container in the driveway.

When we fill our lives with so much stuff, we leave no space for the reality that takes up no space. In our hearts there is no room for relationships, spiritual practice, peace of mind, and contentment. The clutter around us is often a reflection of the clutter within us. Our minds, hearts, and spirits are so cluttered with our stuff and the busyness of it that life revolves around stuff rather than deeper realities. Is it surprising that when we find ourselves in the midst of spring cleaning and unloading some of our old stuff, we find ourselves doing some spring cleaning of the soul as well?

I have always appreciated traveling light through life. I have a rule about stuff: if I don't have room for it in my modest home, something must go. It sure keeps things simpler and allows me to focus on the truly important aspects of life.[54]

—Reverend Catherine Tran

There is a spiritual poverty associated with material affluence. Material possessions can actually become an obstacle to experiencing life more fully. This view was

> *There is a spiritual poverty associated with material affluence. Material possessions can actually become an obstacle to experiencing life more fully.*

espoused by Henry David Thoreau, who wrote eloquently of his austere years living in a hand-built house by Walden Pond.[55] Annie Dillard, the Pulitzer Prize–winning author of *Pilgrim at Tinker Creek*, also spent a year living alone in the woods, cultivating her sense of awe of the natural world and her spirituality, neither of which require owning a lot of stuff.[56] As far back as the Middle Ages, people were moved to give away all their possessions and join the ranks of mendicant friars, devoting their lives to the service of God and His people.

The Opposite of Materialism Is Freedom

My friend Jill spent several seasons as a rafting guide in Alaska. The guides camped in tents all summer, walking into town to fetch food because none of them had a car. Jill had left her car back home in Las Vegas. When she tired of her Alaska experience, she went home to load it up and drive to her next adventure working for a casino in Reno. Two decades later, as she packed the contents of her three-thousand-square-foot house into box after box to be loaded into a moving truck, she lamented no longer being twenty years old and able to stash all her possessions into a hatchback and hit the road, the ultimate freedom.

Indeed, if you want to gain an appreciation of living with minimal possessions and the freedom it accords, shoulder a backpack and set off for some extended travel. Your life will transform into a journey of experience, connection with other human beings, observation of your natural surroundings, and joy in simply being alive.[57]

Experiential Living

Life is what happens when you are busy making plans. Or money. My friend Ann S. spent her adult years living her life with an enviable zest. She managed to arrange her work schedule to take off extended periods of time so she could travel the globe. This included riding her bicycle to Mexico with her brother, spending eighteen months traveling solo through South America, and taking her elderly mother to Greece. For Ann, travel and experiences were vastly more important than material possessions, of which she had few. A coworker advised her early on to set aside 10 percent of her income in savings, which she did faithfully, managing to survive, thrive, and travel frequently on the rest. She is now retired, living comfortably in a $175,000 house for which she paid cash, despite never having netted more than $25,000 per year in her life. Ann's advice to those of us stuck on the corporate treadmill worried about our next raise and promotion: don't forget to live your life while you are earning your living.

Without being fully cognizant that I had done so, I first reached the conclusion that using less does not have to feel like a sacrifice when I went on a trek in the mountains of

Nepal. Traveling in a Third World country, like living off the grid, throws using less in relief. There are a minimum of necessities, and everything else is extraneous. When I talked to the various Westerners I met, I asked them what they missed the most about their own country. No matter whether they had been gone two weeks, two months, or a full year, the number one answer was always the same: flush toilets. Old habits die hard. Squatting may work perfectly well, but if you have been trained to sit and are used to the hygienic aspects of flushing, that's what you crave. It's a comfortable, familiar feeling.

Also high on people's lists were hot and cold running tap water. This was both for taking a steaming hot shower and for having potable water at your fingertips to drink, brush teeth, wash hands, and the myriad other things for which we thoughtlessly use water in industrialized nations.

One person mentioned a warm bedroom. Getting undressed at night in Nepal was chilly and unpleasant at best. At worst I didn't even bother, but crawled into my sleeping bag fully clothed in my sweaty long underwear, cuddling a bottle of boiled water next to me.

Fresh fruit made some people's lists, including mine. I also craved cold milk. The Swiss trekkers brought their own supply of chocolate as protection against inferior varieties, and the English folks mentioned roast beef with Yorkshire pudding. As for me, I had dreams about creamy macaroni and cheese. The other American I met longed for orange juice. Personal preference reigned, but everyone had a food item they craved and simply couldn't get in Nepal.

The curious thing was that absolutely nobody mentioned electricity, television, radio, stereos and CDs (this was pre-MP3 technology), telephones, PDAs, video games, movies, twenty-four-hour news programs, or anything relating to information or nonparticipatory entertainment. One man remarked that he hadn't seen a newspaper in a while, but he didn't say he missed it. With the exception of amenities relating to staying warm and clean, no one mentioned material possessions either. No one missed cars, gadgets, cushy furniture, wall-to-wall carpeting, toys, knickknacks, or any of the plastic junk that fills most of our houses. Eliminating all but the necessities was painless. It freed us up to enjoy the great outdoors and each other's company, two pleasures that cost nothing that I discovered while traveling in Nepal and living off the grid in Taos.

On-grid life can be this uncomplicated too once you release the hold your stuff has on you and instead create a life of a different kind of abundance.

Epilogue

*For my part I know nothing with any certainty, but the
sight of the stars makes me dream.*

—Vincent van Gogh

W HEN I FIRST HAD MY straw bale house in Taos
built, two lawn chairs occupied center stage in the
living room to serve as a couch, with a cooler in between
acting as the coffee table. It was functional in a slightly
uncomfortable way, but I was too cheap to waste money
on actual furniture that would become superfluous when I
ultimately moved in full-time. I am always pleasantly surprised when I make a decision based on a specific motivation (in this case, frugality) and it sends me through an
unanticipated door of possibility.

The lawn chairs, being portable, found their way outside the east side of the house in the morning so I could eat
breakfast with an unobstructed view of Wheeler Peak. In
the evenings, they migrated to the west side of the house
to allow me to watch the sun go down and shadows over-
take the sagebrush. It was a favorite ritual to wind down
from my day. The air cooled off, and nighthawks dived

from hundreds of feet in the air to feast on the insects that swarmed at dusk. Rival bands of coyotes began their nightly war chant.

After it became completely dark, I would adjust my lawn chair to lie flat so I could take in the view straight above. Sometimes I stayed long enough to watch the moon drift across the valley and the stars sprinkle gold dust throughout the night sky. Spending enough time under my own personal heaven allowed me to open up to new ideas as my mind wandered. My house contained very little, and yet I partook of the wealth and abundance that Nature provided in her own way. Life was simplicity itself, and I had never felt more alive.

In Colorado, I had experienced the joy of spending my free time outside playing in gorgeous natural surroundings. But in New Mexico, I developed a much deeper connection to the earth. It was that connection coupled with out-of-the-box, off-the-grid, lawn-chair-furniture thinking that burst apart all the conventional wisdom I had stored in my head from decades of cultural indoctrination. Thirty-seven years of habit was unwound in a matter of months simply by being able to see first-hand the impact of my behavior and purchasing decisions on my natural surroundings.

I believe we can achieve a similar collective unwinding in this country. Old habits may die hard, but new habits bring new possibilities. We as consumers are currently spending our way into the worst kind of debt there is: unrecoverable damage to the planet that is our home.

When you stop and realize that everything you own comes from the earth—the book you are holding, the chair you are sitting on, the clothes you are wearing, the food you ate this morning, the house you live in, the car you drive—it gives you pause. At least, it does for me. I start asking myself questions.

Is it necessary for me to own it, or can I appreciate it merely by looking at it in the store?

Am I using more than my fair share if I buy it?

Did this even need to be produced?

What natural resources were extracted in its production?

What natural resources were discarded in its production?

What by-products, toxic or otherwise, resulted from its manufacture? Where are they now?

How much energy did it take to produce it?

How is that energy itself produced?

Was this item shipped long distances to get to me?

How much energy did that take, and how much pollution did it create?

What is the real cost of this item? Walmart may be able to sell it for $3.50, but that's not the real cost because it doesn't reflect the cost to the earth's natural resources.

Conserving those resources requires all of us to take personal action, however small, in our individual lives. Every little bit counts, and it can all add up to a large impact. In fact, it needs to add up to enough that will allow us to reduce our collective ecological footprint from 1.4 to 1.0, or lower.

You might be of the opinion that it's somebody else's problem to solve. Ken Salazar, the secretary of the interior, declared, "Today there are brilliant, inspired innovators working to make changes as profound in our time as electricity and canals were in their time." Scientists across the globe are hard at work studying everything from nanostructured materials used to enhance the performance of PV devices, to using reclaimed "produced water" from natural gas drilling operations to augment drinking water supplies, to improving the strength and quality of manufactured steel to be used in wind turbine towers.

Good for them, but if none of us does our part, we are wholly reliant on them to pull off a miracle. I'm not willing to take that risk. Besides, I *want* to do my part so I can take credit for helping literally to save the world.

Since I am not a scientist solving the problem by developing new technology to meet future demand, then I can be part of the solution by helping to reduce that demand. As I said before, if you aren't part of the solution, you are part of the problem.

We can wait for the government or academia or industry to accomplish it on a massive scale, or we can take charge of our own consumption habits and achieve it on a personal scale. This is going to require some off-grid thinking.

For example, if you live in a four-thousand-square-foot house (or even a two-thousand-square-foot one), you could consider inviting another family to live with you. Whether or not they share the mortgage as co-owners, pay rent as tenants, or provide cleaning, babysitting, cooking, or dog-walking services in exchange for lodging is up to you. Maybe they provide companionship.

Maybe they are your grandparents. Or your parents. Or your children. Maybe you are a bunch of retirees living in your own personal elder commune. Maybe you are a recent college graduate sharing living space with five of your closest friends. What you are really sharing is the cost of living space and planetary resources. Despite this country's emphasis on independence, there is no shame in not owning your own home, and there are considerable benefits to sharing one.

Despite this country's emphasis on independence, there is no shame in not owning your own home, and there are considerable benefits to sharing one.

My husband and I had a friend and her lapdog live with us for two months in our seven-hundred-square-foot house, along with our new baby and our hundred-pound Weimaraner. She slept on the couch and stored her stuff in our garage. We shared meals with her. In return, she did more house and garden projects than we had a right to expect. Everybody came out a winner.

I can think of another creative solution, this one combining saving energy with getting enough exercise: turn off your TV and spend more time in Nature. Who needs a TV when you have the great outdoors? I grew up running around in the woods of a small mountain town, but you don't actually need that much space to see Nature in action. A friend of mine grew up in suburban

San Antonio. She lived at the end of a cul-de-sac next to an open field, across from which was the town dump. She and her friends spent their waking hours after school playing in that field rather than watching TV.

Another friend was raised in upstate New York before the invention of video games, Tivo, the Internet, or anything else involving a screen that lures you indoors. On the coldest of winter days, she and her little pals would bundle up, strap on their ice skates, and skate around a local pond for hours. They would take breaks to go inside for hot chocolate, then bundle up and do it again.

Children love the outdoors. People in general gravitate toward Nature if given the chance. That's why Central Park is so popular in New York City. Imagine what a loss it would be if they ever decide to pave over that park. If you are shocked at the very idea, then you are a Nature lover. Welcome to the club.

No matter where you live, you can find a green spot to enjoy or cultivate and nurture, even if it's only the tomatoes in a pot on your fire escape. The Greatest Generation, as Tom Brokaw called them, grew vegetables as a matter of course during World War II out of a sense of duty to their country. Our generation can do the same out of a sense of duty to the planet. The stakes are as high now as they have ever been.

So slow down a bit. Take the time to sit out on that fire escape with the tomatoes and watch the world go by. Even in a city you may thrill to see a hawk, or you might enjoy watching the pigeons or squirrels. In the suburbs you will probably see foxes and coyotes, which are very adaptable animals.

We're adaptable animals too. We've gone from being conservationists during World War II to consumers in the new millennium, but we can adapt our way back. Talk to anyone over the age of seventy about their conservation ethic and ask them how we can get it back. We can save the planet, and we might just save a little money as well.

Our Self-Sustaining Planet

These days when I walk into a room, I turn the light on automatically, even during the day if the room is dim. I would never have done that in my house in Taos. As long as I could see just a little, the light stayed off. The reason was simple: I was paranoid about running out of electricity because we had sized my PV system for weekend, not full-time, use. Living there full-time, I was using more resources than my house could support, much more than it was designed for. Running out was inevitable if I didn't conserve.

To maintain an equilibrium, energy used had to equal energy generated. But I started at a disadvantage because of my initial underestimation of how much I would use. From the beginning of my year off the grid, energy used exceeded energy generated if I didn't conserve. Because the energy generated never increased, when I added population in the form of guests, it put a massive strain on the system, and I ran out of power and water even more quickly.

In 2009, humans on the planet collectively used 1.4 times the amount of resources that the earth can sustain long-term. If we continue without modifying our conservation and consumption behavior, running out is inevitable. This is true even without accounting for population increases.

> *In 2009, humans on the planet collectively used 1.4 times the amount of resources that the earth can sustain long-term. If we continue without modifying our conservation and consumption behavior, running out is inevitable.*

If we do account for them—the earth's population is expected to hit nine billion by the year 2040, according to the U.S. Census Bureau—we will run out even sooner because of the massive strain put on the system.

That makes my house rather like the earth in microcosm. They are both self-sustaining entities. They both produce their own energy and water and neutralize their own waste. They both have a finite amount of resources to draw upon. And they both have fluctuating demands placed on those resources because of variable populations.

In my house, you don't want to squander your energy by leaving unnecessary lights on, or your heat by leaving the front door open, or your water by letting the tap run continuously while you do the dishes. You want to pay single-minded attention to all of your actions and make decisions that will conserve, not consume, those precious resources.

Sometimes it was annoying not to be guaranteed that the lights would come on when I flipped the switch. Especially after visiting on-grid friends, I would return to Taos a little disgruntled at not being able to turn on all the lights, play a CD, charge my cell phone, and use my food processor all at once for fear of having it suddenly cut off. My friends indiscriminately used power without thinking about it, without worrying that its source was slowly being drawn down, without trying to conserve it until they were confident it had been replenished.

The irony, of course, is that it their situation was the same as mine, only they didn't see it illustrated so dramatically on a daily basis, because they are removed from the source of all the resources they used. Because I lived in a house where I could see the finite quantity of my electricity in my batteries, my heat in my woodpile, and my water in my cistern, I was faced every day with the reality of conservation. If I didn't conserve, I would run out.

The same situation exists for everyone on earth: if we don't conserve our resources, we will run out. In my house in Taos, we can't predict what that will look like. For me, the lights suddenly extinguish when I am out of power, or the gauge on the pressure tank drops slowly until it hits zero and I have no more water. For the planet, who knows?

But here's the good news: if we all contribute a little, each according to his or her means, the solution may be greater than the sum of its parts. If all you can do is conserve water, then conserve water. If you can take public transportation instead of driving to work every day, then do that. If you can afford to cover your roof with solar panels and sell power to the national grid, then I believe you have an obligation to do so. Whatever you can do, you should do. We are all in this together.

Even so, certain people could stand to do a little more than others. If you are living hand-to-mouth, you probably already buy less stuff and use less energy to heat your small home than your wealthier counterparts.

One creative idea to reduce global carbon emissions was postulated in a paper published in the *Proceedings of the National Academy of Sciences* in July 2009. It suggested that instead of rich *countries* reducing their greenhouse gas emissions (the focus of current policy suggestions), it was rich *people* who needed to alter their behavior. The authors hypothesized that if international bodies set a target cap on total emissions and converted it into a per-person cap for all people on the planet, we could collectively meet the global target as long as everyone stuck to their personal limit.

This way, the very rich people in countries with large numbers of poor people (for example, China and India), couldn't leverage off their fellow citizens to continue their wasteful, high-consumption lifestyles.

The authors gave examples with numbers to illustrate their idea. If, for example, the global cap were set at thirty billion metric tons by 2030, then 1.1 billion people globally would need to change their behavior. Each country could enforce its own citizens' consumption patterns however they chose. In America, most of us would need to make some changes.

The Path to Victory

Before you get defensive, recall that your grandparents knew how to conserve when we shared the goal of winning the Second World War. That global conflict left our country with the spoils of war, reinterpreted for peacetime: an explosion of pesticides and insecticides derived from the chemicals formerly used to make war; tasteless, unhealthy, manufactured food of the same type used to feed our soldiers on the front lines (just add water!); and—on the plus side—a conservation ethic on the home front. Reduce, reuse, recycle was a way of life for an entire generation before the slogan was adopted fifty years later.

The Greatest Generation (whatever that means) made personal short-term sacrifices for the good of the country and emerged victorious. In the name of patriotism, citizens of the United States subjected themselves to the rationing of consumer goods, cutting back on necessities and denying themselves a lot of the niceties that we take for granted today.

Even before the war, Americans lacked most of the niceties that we consider necessities today, and yet we were still considered a prosperous nation. For example, it was only in the late 1800s that indoor plumbing became available, and it wasn't common in homes until the mid-20th century. (In postwar Europe, it was later than that.)

What would you do without running water? Olive doesn't have it, nor does she complain that she is deprived. Most people I talk to visibly cringe when I mention her lack of indoor plumbing. Olive herself clearly has no problem stepping outdoors with a flashlight on a cold winter's evening to use her doorless outhouse while looking at the constellations wheeling overhead.

But most people declare they could never live that way. I assume they mean not voluntarily, although I bet they would—voluntarily—if the motivation were great enough. I think the reason they believe they couldn't live without an indoor toilet is one of the following three:

1. **Fear: They don't currently live without indoor plumbing and never have.** Plenty of people are apprehensive about the unknown.

2. **Desire: They don't want to. This simply boils down to motivation.** If you were to change

the purpose of your life and go volunteer at an orphanage in Nepal, for example, I bet you would willingly and without complaint do your business in an outhouse.

3. **Entitlement: They don't think they should have to.** This is pure arrogance. Just because we have had indoor plumbing in America for several generations' lifetimes doesn't mean we always will. If you plot our current population growth and water consumption, project them against our finite available water resources, throw in the effects of global warming (e.g., less snowfall), and refuse to do anything about it, you might reach the conclusion that American households won't have continuous, on-demand, running water in the future, particularly in the West. If we reach that state, Olive will continue her life with no impact, as will that orphanage in Nepal. The rest of us will have some adjustments to make.

Today we have another worthwhile goal that requires conservation: saving the earth's resources and preserving them for our descendants and the other inhabitants of the planet. It may not feel as urgent as winning a war because the consequences of our behavior have a longer time horizon to play out, but it is still supremely important.

America is by far the greatest consumer of resources per capita on the planet. We consume, we waste, we discard. We can't forget, however, that we're all in it together as citizens of planet earth. We are neighbors to countries, people, animals, and plants. Our actions affect their well-being. It's time to start thinking long-term.

What will your great-great-great-grandchildren's lives be like? Think carefully of them the next time you buy a microwaveable dinner or a new TV.

The solution to our planetary woes is the same as it was for our country during World War II: use less. It's quite simple.

Stop watching the news that labels you a consumer and start thinking of yourself as a conserver. Better yet, think of yourself as a citizen of the planet, responsible for its conservation. If you can visualize its finite energy (stored in oil fields), its finite water (stored in oceans, surface water, and ground water), and its other finite resources (rainforests, fertile land, plant and animal species) every time you want to make a purchase, I guarantee you will make those purchases differently or not at all.

When I make all these declarations about conservation to some people, their reaction is, "That's all right for you, but I could never do it." They think they can't do it because they have children or elderly parents or an image to maintain or Responsibilities. What they are really saying is they are afraid of change. They have a litany of unspoken questions that reflect their fears, but they can all be challenged.

> What if I try using less stuff and it is too much of
> a sacrifice? *What if you got laid off and didn't have a
> choice? Better to do it on your own terms.*

> What if I change my consumer habits, and my
> spouse/children/family/neighbors/friends/colleagues
> lose respect for me? *What if you turn out to be a role
> model for them?*

> What if I find out I'm not good at conserving,
> because consuming has been my status quo for so

long? *What if you find that you are fantastic at it? You never know until you try.*

What if everybody stops buying stuff and the American economy grinds to a halt? *Then we will have busted the myth that continuous growth is good or even possible. And you will be prepared to live on less because you will already know how to do it.*

Change can be volatile, I will be the first to admit. During the last two years at my corporate job before I quit and moved to Taos, I'm sure I got a reputation as the office hippie. I fit in less and less as I aligned my life with my values, and I know it made some people uncomfortable. They had to take a look at themselves and their values when I became different enough. It was difficult for me too, being surrounded by people who didn't share my way of thinking.

Once I quit, though, and started living those values, my psyche settled down and my conscience was at ease. The throes of change are turbulent, but if you make it through to the other side, you find calmer waters.

There is nothing to fear—not change, not the unknown—as long as you are prepared to be flexible. As Franklin Delano Roosevelt said during his first inaugural address in 1933, "the only thing we have to fear is fear itself: nameless, unreasoning, unjustified terror which paralyzes needed efforts to convert retreat into advance." It's time to be fearless and advance.

What Can You Do?

My friend Jill is worried that too many people will read this book, be partial to its principles, and decide to move to Taos. That would be a tragedy since most of the problems brought up in these pages stem from overpopulation. It would also be a tragedy if people moved here and brought their mainstream ideas with them. Taos is not a mainstream place. You have to have at least one screw loose to live here (by mainstream definition, not by ours). This is a place of artists and writers, native musicians and medicine women, kayakers and climbers, Telemarkers and fly fishermen, environmentalists and peace activists, organic farmers and beekeepers, weavers and carvers, chefs and shopkeepers, hippies and tenth-generation Hispanics, Pueblo Indians and gringos, yoga instructors, and Buddhists.

If you stand in the center of town and throw a stone (which we don't encourage because we're nonviolent) or swing a dead cat (also frowned upon for obvious reasons), you will hit someone who hasn't bathed since last week, or who makes his own rose hip tea, or who is building her own house without benefit of building codes or inspectors, or who just got back from a month of meditation in Bhutan, or whose paintings are in a gallery in Paris, or whose ancestors have lived here four times as long as this country is old. We like it that way.

But I have more confidence than Jill. I think that the people who like what they read in this book and are ready for a change will decide to make a difference in their own communities. It takes people to build a culture, and your culture, where you live, includes your influence. Exert it a little more.

It takes people to build a culture, and your culture, where you live, includes your influence. Exert it a little more.

Do you want an artistic community in your area? Create one. Do you want a farmers' market in your city? Start one. Do you want to build an off-grid house in an urban area? Make it happen. All you need are a couple of like-minded people and some determination.

There are two ways to effect change in America: from the top down, and from the bottom up. If enough people seek out farmers' markets for fresh, locally grown, organic produce, the sheer demand will create more farmers' markets. That's bottom up. If building the straw bale home of your dreams is not permitted by local building codes, lobby for a waiver or a regulation change. You may set a precedent to pave the way for others to follow. That's top down.

There is no problem that cannot be solved with a little creativity. Money is never the only solution; don't let a lack of it stop you. For example, if you want to improve the environment in your city, you could operate on a small scale and replace your lawn with indigenous plants. If you live in an apartment building, ask permission to grow plants on the roof (right next to the solar panels you talk them into installing). Or you could think bigger and come up with an idea like the one I have for Colorado Springs to connect the many parks and open spaces by bike and pedestrian paths.

There are probably many compelling reasons that you live where you do. Maybe your family is there, you own an affordable house, you like your job (or you can't leave it for some reason), you like the weather, or you're a fan of the baseball team. So stay there and make it better. You have the power.

What can you do? The list is long, the choices many. The general idea is to pick one and continue it until it becomes a habit, then observe how making even one change will conserve multiple resources, including, often, your own money.

Here are just a few ideas:

Heat

- Turn your heat off or down significantly enough that you need to dramatically alter your behavior to stay warm. Put a sweater on, curl up with the dog, huddle under a down comforter, or simply acclimate to the cold. Do this for a weekend and make note of the things you do to stay warm. Continue doing them after you turn your heat back up (but only a wee bit).

- Apply passive solar principles to your home, or find a new home. (Don't build a new one.)

- Insulate, insulate, insulate, and plug all leaks.

Power and Light

- Turn off all electric appliances for a full day, week, month, or whatever you can handle, and see where you conserve. Then continue the practice. Notice the effect on your utility bill and bank the savings.

- Turn off your lights when not in use to enjoy natural light and darkness.

- Don't replace your electric appliances when they break: share someone else's instead. For example, do your laundry at a Laundromat, watch TV in a public setting, use the computer at a public library or Internet café.

- If you have the wherewithal to buy solar panels, a home-sized wind turbine, or a different homegrown source of energy, produce more power than you use. Sell excess power back to the grid, if your local utility company allows it.

- Exert pressure on local, state, and federal authorities to require a higher percentage of utility companies' power to come from renewable resources. Vote for any measure that supports this idea.

Water

- Get rid of your lawn if you have one.

- Do fewer loads of laundry and dishes by using clothes and dishes more than once before washing them.

- Shower less frequently than daily.

- Try using only the water you can carry for a weekend and see where you decide to conserve, then continue that practice.

- Share water resources; for example, at a Laundromat, a park, or public pool.

Food

- Grow your own, whether that means herbs on a windowsill or full-scale crops in the backyard.

- Participate in a Community Supported Agriculture (CSA) food co-op.

- Buy in bulk from farmers' markets and then can or freeze the produce for winter use.

- Buy from local producers, even in the supermarket. Ask your grocer where they get their produce, meat, and dairy products.

- If farmers' markets or CSAs don't exist in your area, help create them.

- Try guerrilla gardening—surreptitiously planting food crops in public spaces such as medians or vacant lots. Or just plant flowers as your own personal carbon offset and public beautification program.

Garbage

- Cancel your trash service (or simply don't use it) for a month and see how you cope, then continue those practices.

- Recycle everything. If your municipality doesn't pick it up at your door, find out where to take it and do so. Pressure everyone to recycle, from your local coffee shop to your city's football stadium to public gathering spots.

- Compost. If you can't use it, find out who can and take it there.

- Stop buying packaged food.

- Scrutinize your purchases and make only those with limited packaging, or make fewer purchases in general.

- Lobby lawmakers to require manufacturers to use less packaging to begin with.

Transportation

- Don't drive your car for a week and notice how you get around. Carpool? Bike? Walk? Bus? Train? Car share? Keep doing that. Then maybe get rid of your car and its associated bills.

- Walk or bike everywhere. Support local businesses and shed a few pounds. Ditch your gym membership.

- Stay put. Slow down your life and enjoy being at home and all the places within walking distance.

Stuff

- Declare a "material fast" for a month and see if you really needed all that stuff you were tempted to buy. Shrink your credit card bills in the process.

- Put off purchases as long as possible, maybe even forever if you eventually decide you don't really need whatever it is you were going to buy.

- Stop shopping as a hobby.

- Share big-ticket items with a neighbor or friend: lawn mowers, snow blowers, tools, or anything you use infrequently.

- Move to a smaller home and scale down your life.

- Stop trying to impress people with your possessions. Dazzle them with your fiscal and environmental brilliance instead.

Years ago, the TV show *Saturday Night Live* (or, more accurately, the comedian Dana Carvey) did an impression of then president George Bush. The punch line, based on a favorite saying of the president's, was invariably "wouldn't be prudent, wouldn't be prudent," no matter what the political dilemma. We seem to have strayed from prudence into heavy risk-taking, both with our finances and the fate of the planet.

Scientific consensus confirms that the earth is warming and that most of the temperature rise can be correlated to human activity, which has caused a striking increase in the emission of greenhouse gases since the Industrial Revolution. There still seem to be people who doubt this, who think global warming is a myth. To them I offer my standard conservative advice: in the absence of good information or the presence of conflicting information, act prudently. In the case of climate change, this means cutting back on the production of greenhouse gases. That correlates nicely with using less of the planet's resources.

To offer an analogy, if you want to know whether you will need a jacket to stay warm when you go outside, and two weather forecasters are predicting two different temperatures, the conservative thing to do is to take a jacket just in case. Leaving the house without one wouldn't be prudent. It's easy to do, and there is no risk in doing it. To me, conservation is a similar easy, risk-free decision.

I know I'm a dreamer. I also know I made my own dreams come true by bucking convention. Collectively, we can kick the habit of so-called conventional wisdom, apply a little off-grid thinking, and make the planet of our dreams come true. We can create anew our world of no pollution, fresh air, clean water, and an abundance of natural resources. We can restore green fields of healthful foods and grazing animals with plenty of space. We can recycle all waste productively. The wild animals will have room to roam, the ocean will rebuild its stocks of fish, and skies will contain a profusion of birds.

All it takes is a little judicious action and conservation on the part of enough motivated people. We can slow down our lives, destress, and find satisfaction in the grace of everyday living. Or we can bet that the earth's resources can handle the demand of an ever-increasing population that is greedy to continue our current patterns of consumption. I don't know about you, but I believe continuing the wasteful status quo wouldn't be intelligent. Nor would it be conservative, sensible, or rational. In short, it wouldn't be prudent.

Notes

Chapter 1: A Different Way of Life

1. There are multitudes of carbon and ecological footprint calculators available online. They probably all do the job just fine but use different algorithms, which means you will get different results from each one. It doesn't matter. All you need is a ballpark figure, especially if you can compare your footprint to the average American's and the average for people living in different countries. A couple to try are the one from the EPA (*www.epa.gov/climatechange/emissions/ind_calculator.html*), one from the Nature Conservancy (*www.nature.org/initiatives/climatechange/calculator*), and one from the Earth Day Network (*www.earthday.org*).

2. The United Nations Statistics Division (*unstats.un.org/unsd/default.htm*) is responsible for providing official global statistics on everything from economics to geography to the environment. They make an effort to provide standardized statistics so that countries can be compared in an "apples to apples" sort of way. Their website is a gold mine of information.

3. Charlie's company, Natural Builders, can be found at *www.naturalbuildersllc.com*. In addition to a description of their building and remodeling services and a gallery of lovely pictures, they also have a link to an energy modeling website where you can find more information about solar design than you probably thought you wanted to know.

4. Joaquin's company, Zero E Design, can be found at *www.zeroedesign.com*. There is a photo gallery of his projects that

shows how beautiful sustainable architecture can be. If you click on "The Team" link and read Joaquin's biography, you will find an interesting note at the end that effectively declares passive solar design to be "so '90s." As effective as it is, there are more cutting-edge approaches on the horizon, such as the European Passive house concept. Houses built under this design standard differ from traditional passive solar homes by recovering heat from internal sources (e.g., waste heat from lights, appliances, and even body heat) and exchanging it with fresh air to maintain a comfortable interior temperature without the use of active heating mechanisms.

5. *The Straw Bale House*, by Athena Swentzell Steen, Bill Steen, and David Bainbridge (Chelsea Green Publishing Company, 1994) was my inspiration and bible when it came to designing and building my straw bale house. It champions a can-do spirit and has beautiful photographs of straw bale homes.

Chapter 2: Heat

6. For more information on homes built for free heating and cooling, see *The Passive Solar House: Using Solar Design to Heat & Cool Your Home*, by James Kachadorian (Chelsea Green Publishing Company, 1997). This was one of the books that inspired me to build off the grid in the first place. It taught me that central heating is unnecessary if you orient your house properly.

7. Bandelier National Monument's website, *www.nps.gov/band/index.htm*, gives you all the information you need to visit this fascinating, beautiful place in the mountains of New Mexico.

8. If you are an overdomesticated adult, it is fully within your power to expose yourself more to the natural world. But if you are a child, particularly one who lives in a city, you might need some help. That's what the Fresh Air Fund provides. You can find them at *www.freshair.org/*.

9. For solid, standard advice on how to save energy in your home and money on your heating bill, check out the Department of Energy's website at *www.energysavers.gov/your_home/space_heating_cooling/index.cfm/mytopic=12300*.

10. As long ago as 1998, Sarah Susanka published a book called *The Not So Big House: A Blueprint for the Way We Really Live* (Taunton Press), adjuring us to build smaller but smarter. After a decade of largely ignoring her advice, our country is finally getting the message. However, remodeling rather than building new is still the most economically viable option for most people and the most environmentally friendly way to go. Hence, her latest book, *Not So Big Remodeling: Tailoring Your Home for the Way You Really Live*, with Marc Vassallo (Taunton Press, 2009).

11. Want to retrofit your home with straw bales? It can be done. See the overview article "Retrofitting a House with Straw Bales" on *StrawBale.com*. (*www.strawbale.com/retrofitting-a-house-with-straw-bales*)

12. When I traveled to Iceland and took a tour of the spectacular natural wonders they have, my bus driver tour guide informed me that Iceland intended to be the world's first pollution-free country. I didn't doubt him, but I did verify the claim on both the BBC ("Iceland launches energy revolution," *news.bbc.co.uk/2/hi/science/nature/1727312.stm*) and CNN ("Iceland phasing out fossil fuels for clean energy," *www.cnn.com/2007/TECH/science/09/18/driving.iceland/index.html*). It's a lofty goal that I hope they achieve.

13. For information on backup heat sources, visit *www.russianstove.com* or *www.epa.gov/air/burnwise*, the Environmental Protection Agency's site listing the woodstoves, inserts, and pellet stoves that meet their pollution emission ratings. But don't confuse emission ratings with efficiency. Maximizing efficiency is up to you and is a function of your choice of fuel and how well you build your fire.

Chapter 3: Power and Light

14. If you are interested the effects of light pollution, check out the website of the International Dark-Sky Association, *www .darksky.org*.

15. See the Energy Information Administration's report "How Much Coal Is Left" at *tonto.eia.doe.gov/energyexplained/index .cfm?page=coal_reserves*. The EIA, the Department of Energy's statistical and analytical agency, online at *tonto.eia.doe.gov*, is the go-to website for official energy statistics.

16. Do you know where your power comes from? The National Public Radio website features an interactive map ("Visualizing the U.S. Electric Grid," *www.npr.org/templates/story/story .php?storyId=110997398*) that illustrates the interconnected grids, power plant locations, and each state's sources of power (e.g., coal, oil, natural gas, wind, solar, hydro, and biomass).

Chapter 4: Water

17. The Council for Environmental Education has produced an instructional guide aimed at schoolchildren to teach them how to read a water bill as part of water consumption awareness. If you are looking for simple instructions to figure out how to read your meter and calculate your consumption, check it out at *www.wetcity.org/resources/Read a Water Meter and Water Bill.pdf*. Of course, you can always call your water provider and have them walk you through your bill. Some of it is more complicated than you think, including tiered rate structures and fixed charges unrelated to water use.

18. To investigate your local drinking water, visit the EPA's "How to Access Local Drinking Water Information" at *www .epa.gov/safewater/databases/sdwis/howtoaccessdata.html*.

19. The *New York Times* series Toxic Waters and its roundup of website resources for "anyone seeking to learn more about water quality, pollution, or how to evaluate or treat their drinking water" can be found at *projects.nytimes.com/toxic-waters*.

20. To find the right water filter for your home, check out the Natural Resources Defense Council's consumer guide at *www.nrdc.org/water/drinking/gfilters.asp.*

21. There are many ways to find xeriscaping resources. Local utility companies sometimes offer information or classes, such as the one my friend Frank took through Colorado Springs Utilities. Also, your local botanic garden can be a tremendous resource. In my area, the Denver Botanic Gardens have a xeric demonstration garden and a page on their website devoted to selecting xeric plants for this region. See *www .botanicgardens.org/.*

22. One way to find options for low-water-use plants that will thrive in your area is to seek information from your state's nearest Cooperative Extension office. Cooperative Extensions are educational offices at each state's land-grant university or universities that provide agricultural information to farmers, ranchers, students, consumers, and anyone else with a question. The USDA National Institute of Food and Agriculture has a web page to help you locate your local Cooperative Extension, found here: *www.csrees.usda.gov/Extension/.* Click on your state and search for "low-water-use plants," or contact them directly to ask them what low-water-use plants might best suit your region.

23. If you also live in the West or Southwest in an arid and high-altitude climate, visit High Country Gardens' website, *www.highcountrygardens.com,* to find the kinds of plants that are suitable for that climate and look for them in your local nursery. If you are local to Santa Fe, Santa Fe Greenhouses (*santafegreenhouses.com*), High Country Greenhouse's retail location, is definitely worth a visit.

24. To discover how much water you use and how to conserve it, use the H_2O Conserve Water Footprint Calculator on the GRACE Communication Foundation website at *www .h2oconserve.org/home.php?pd=index.*

25. See "There's a water war on the Colorado-Wyoming border, and Aaron Million is quick on the draw," by Joel Warner,

November 26, 2009. Available online at *www.westword*
.com/content/printVersion/1332262/.

26. See page 5 of "Colorado Statewide Water Supply Initiative,"
by Kelly DiNatale, et al, of CDM (American Water Works
Association, 2005), available online at *www.cdm.com/NR/*
rdonlyres/0ED27922-DFB9-431F-A9DF-4328B0CE3FC4/0/
ColoradoStatewideWaterSupplyInitiative.pdf.

27. Water quality and regulation is an issue on federal, state,
and local levels. The Department of the Interior has a role in
water management, although I haven't been able to determine
whether they or any government entity has ultimate authority
over a coordinated water policy for the country. Their "Water
Challenges" web page (*www.doi.gov/whatwedo/water/*) lists
all the great things they are doing but leaves me scratching
my head as to who is in charge. I did find a private organization called WaterWired that posted a blog entry on December 8, 2008, which offered a "Roadmap for Future U.S. Global
Water Policy. It's interesting reading: *aquadoc.typepad.com/*
waterwired/2008/12/roadmap-for-future-us-water-policy.html.
Individual states also seem to have water policy organizations.
For example, the state of Colorado has a Division of Water
Resources that publishes the SWSI report, the latest of which
is located at *water.state.co.us/pubs/swsi.asp*.

Chapter 5: Food

28. For those of you who, like me, don't have much of a green
thumb but are willing to learn, you can always try "WWOOF-
ing." Willing Workers on Organic Farms has an excellent website to match up willing workers with organic farms all over the
world: *www.wwoof.com*.

29. To calculate your food's carbon emissions, an overlooked
source when calculating carbon footprints, use the Low
Carbon Diet Calculator at *www.eatlowcarbon.org/*. Bon Appétit
magazine's Conscious Cook blog (*www.bonappetit.com/*
blogsandforums/blogs/consciouscook) has information on eating
"greener, simpler, and healthier."

30. The USDA gives the official government definition of *organic* along with their organic standards at *www.usda.gov.*

31. The Environmental Working Group (*www.ewg.org/*), is a nonprofit group that updates its website regularly with "The Dirty Dozen": the dozen fruits and vegetables that are most likely to contain pesticide residue. They also list those that are least likely to contain it. See their regularly updated list at *www.foodnews.org/fulllist.php.*

32. Two great organizations, Seed Savers Exchange (*www .seedsavers.org*) and Baker Creek Heirloom Seeds (*rareseeds .com*), will sell you seeds of heirloom plants if you are looking for old, reliable, tasty varieties and want to preserve garden bio-diversity while you are at it.

33. If you don't have a backyard big enough to plant a garden (or don't have one at all), see an incredible assortment of small space garden ideas at *Sunset Magazine*'s website, *www.sunset .com/garden/.* For an even smaller space, try Woolly Pockets: *www.woollypocket.com.*

34. SPIN Farming makes commercial farming accessible to anyone, even those without land. Check out *spinfarming.com* for information on urban community farming and a shift in mindset for what farming means.

35. Modern foragers should check out *www.neighborhoodfruit .com* and *www.veggietrader.com* for resources in "urban forag-ing," meaning fruits and vegetables growing in cities that are available for the taking or exchange. For example, we have three apple trees on our property right now and don't do much with the fruit beyond bake a pie or two. The rest goes to waste. Somebody, please eat it.

36. To find a Community Supported Agriculture farm or a farmers' market near you, see *www.localharvest.org.*

37. *The Flexitarian Diet: The Mostly Vegetarian Way to Lose Weight, Be Healthier, Prevent Disease, and Add Years to Your Life,* by Dawn Jackson Blatner (McGraw-Hill, 2010). Dawn Jackson Blatner is a self-admitted "closet meat-eater," which is why I

like her. Her book offers strategies to move toward vegetarian-ism, a way of eating that is healthier for humans and the planet, even if you can't bring yourself to go all the way.

Chapter 6: Garbage

38. To see what kind of mess foreign climbers and trekkers have made of Mount Everest, go to *www.extremeeverestexpedition .com/*, the website of one of the clean-up missions. On a related note, the late Sir Edmund Hillary set up the Himalayan Trust, a charity that benefits the Sherpas of Nepal. The trust's website is *www.himalayantrust.co.uk.*

39. If you don't already recycle and would like to start, first call your garbage company and see what they offer. If they don't recycle all the items you would like them to, or if you'd rather not pay for their services, store your recyclables in your own bins and periodically take them to a recycling center. To locate a recycling center near you, go to *http://search.earth911.com/.*

40. Information on Germany's Recycling and Waste Act can be found at *www.sfs-dortmund.de/smac/EnviAct1.html.* You can also read an article on their exemplary and effective recy-cling and waste management efforts at *http://earth911.com/ news/2009/07/13/trash-planet-germany/.*

41. If you are a data junkie like me and dry government statis-tics interest you, then you will enjoy the EPA's garbage page on their website: *www.epa.gov/osw/nonhaz/municipal/index.htm.* Only they don't call it garbage; they call it municipal solid waste (MSW). If you have ever worked for the government, you know that giving something a fancy title and an acronym is standard operating procedure (SOP).

42. If you would like to build your own composter, see *http:// seattletilth.org/learn/resources-1/compost* for information on how to go about it. You can find general composting information and resources at Compostable Organics Out of Landfills by 2012 (*www.cool2012.com*). To find a place near you that will take compostable material, compost it, and (typically) sell the

finished compost, check out *www.findacomposter.com*. Or if you are more of a bookworm (pun intended), read the simple but inspiring *Worms Eat My Garbage*, by Mary Appelhof (Flower Press, 1997).

43. If building a house with garbage—the ultimate zero-impact, reuse model—appeals to you, go to the website of the Greater World Earthship community at *http://earthship.com*. You can learn most of what you need online or find a workshop to take. And if you are ever in the Taos area, spend an hour at their demonstration home to open your mind to a completely different way of living.

44. Part of recycling is not just donating your material but also using recycled or "lightly used" stuff. An excellent place to start if you are building or remodeling a house is the Habitat for Humanity ReStore, which sells reusable building materials. To find a ReStore near you to shop for or donate materials, visit *www.habitat.org/env/restores.aspx*.

45. Olive has a website, *www.o-LiveLand.com*, where you can see pictures of the jewelry she makes from found objects. If you have found a few objects that you think would go nicely in a necklace, email her.

46. There is a whole artistic subculture devoted to creating art out of trash. Start at *www.webdesignerdepot.com/2009/12/non-trashy-recycled-and-trash-art/* and see where your clicks lead you.

47. Like I said, it's all sacred ground. Listen to "Sacred Ground," music and lyrics by Laura Wilson and CB Eagye, from Laura Wilson's debut CD *Kicking the Tires*, on YouTube at *www.youtube.com/watch?v=dS6jziTIzJo*, or search "Sacred Ground Laura Wilson" using your Internet browser.

Chapter 7: Transportation

48. *Desert Solitaire: A Season in the Wilderness*, by Edward Abbey (Ballantine Books, 1968; reprint edition Touchstone, 1990). In this classic environmental screed, Abbey rails against roads in national parks and tells a rollicking good tale to boot.

49. Government websites are great for standard definitions and basic information. The Department of Energy's site is no exception. See *www.energysavers.gov/your_vehicle* for alternative fuel vehicle information.

50. If you decide to cut down on driving by carpooling, eRideShare (*www.erideshare.com/*), Carpool Connect (*www.carpoolconnect.com*), and Carpool World (*www.carpoolworld.com*) are just a few websites that can help you find a carpool. By the way, carpooling doesn't just refer to commuting. You can also find rideshares for a one-time journey, whether it is across the country at Thanksgiving or to the next town over for the weekend.

51. There are bike-share programs all over the world. I used one in Munich (very efficient) and saw a similar one in Oslo (very clean). The first such program in the United States, B-cycle, is located in Denver. See their website at *www.bcycle.com* and vote online to have them choose your city as their next location for expansion.

52. Visit ZipCar's website at *www.zipcar.com*. If you are planning on traveling to Europe, check whether they have cars in any of your destination cities. Signing up for ZipCar might actually be cheaper than renting a car.

Chapter 8: Stuff

53. To give and receive your stuff for free, check out *www.freecycle.org*. Or visit the old stand-bys, Goodwill (*www.goodwill.org/*) and the Salvation Army (*www.salvationarmyusa.org*), to find local drop-off locations where you can donate all that clutter you are getting rid of. One man's trash is another man's treasure, and the proceeds go to a worthy cause.

54. Reverend Catherine Tran, who wrote this sidebar, runs a website called *www.creativespirituality.net* where she offers online retreats in addition to her insightful and eminently readable blog.

55. One of the earliest and best-known American gurus of simple living was Henry David Thoreau, who spent two years

living in a house he built himself on his friend Ralph Waldo Emerson's property on the shores of Walden Pond. He chronicled his experiment in his book *Walden; or, Life in the Woods*, first published in 1854.

56. Annie Dillard spent a year living by Tinker Creek and writing about her ascetic and spiritual experience, a more modern take on Thoreau's experiment. The fruit of her labor, *Pilgrim at Tinker Creek* (Bantom, 1975), won her a Pulitzer Prize. Incidentally, Dillard wrote her master's thesis on Thoreau's *Walden*.

57. If you think you can't chuck it all and go traveling because you have a family, think again. Soultravelers3 (*http:// soultravelers3.com/*), the online journal of a family traveling around the world with their five-year-old daughter, shows you how possible it is.

Further Resources

Affluenza: The All-Consuming Epidemic, 2nd ed., by John de Graaf, David Wann, and Thomas H. Naylor (Berrett-Koehler, 2005). The authors define "affluenza" as "a painful, contagious, socially transmitted condition of overload, debt, anxiety, and waste resulting from the dogged pursuit of more." That just about sums it up.

Cadillac Desert: The American West and Its Disappearing Water, by Marc Reisner (Penguin, 1993). As far back as 1993, people were pointing out how flawed water policy and politics influence the quantity, quality, and accessibility of water in the American West. This book is a classic.

"The Conservation Esthetic," *The Sand County Almanac, and Sketches Here and There*, by Aldo Leopold (Oxford University Press, 1949). This classic take on conservation was radical in its time.

Food Rules: An Eater's Manual, by Michael Pollan (Penguin, 2009). This book contains sixty-four very simple rules for eating a healthful diet. My favorite is "Don't eat ingredients that you wouldn't cook with."

"The Global Energy Challenge," by Roel Snieder (public lecture), *inside.mines.edu/~rsnieder/Global_Energy.html*. Since I live in Colorado now, I encounter research and publications from my state's colleges and universities, such as this lecture by Colorado School of Mines professor Roel Snieder.

Home Power Magazine, *http://homepower.com/home/*. Founded in 1987, this print and online publication is a terrific general resource for people interested in building or converting homes to provide their own power. They have been doing it for so long they really know what they are talking about.

Homemade Money: How to Save Energy and Dollars in Your Home, by Richard Heede and the staff of Rocky Mountain Institute (Brickhouse, 1995). If you don't want to go to the extreme of producing your own power but still want to conserve energy (and money), this practical guide has plenty of suggestions.

How to Live Well Without Owning a Car: Save Money, Breathe Easier, and Get More Mileage Out of Life, by Chris Balish (Ten Speed Press, 2006). If you like to bike and live in a city, this guide to car-free living is for you. The title says it all.

"Locavore Nation," The Splendid Table, *http://splendidtable .publicradio.org/locavore_nation/.* According to their website, "Locavore Nation was a year-long effort in 2008 to see what it takes to live by a regionally based diet." It provides an entertaining, funny, and inspirational look at ways to eat locally and affordably.

The Long Emergency: Surviving the End of Oil, Climate Change, and Other Converging Catastrophes of the Twenty-First Century, by James Howard Kunstler (Grove Press, 2006). This book presents a doom-and-gloom worst-case scenario for energy consumption and the End of Life as We Know It. It's worth a read, especially if you need to be scared into action, and could prove to be laughably inaccurate if we all start conserving now.

Natural Home magazine, *http://www.naturalhomemagazine.com/.* This magazine and its website are other good general resources for all things environmental involving your house.

The Rocky Mountain Institute, *www.rmi.org.* According to their forward-thinking, innovative, and informative website, RMI's "vision is a world thriving, verdant, and secure, for all, for ever." Among other things, they focus on a concept they call "natural capitalism," which has to do with economic progress that reverses our current trend of consuming the earth's diminishing natural capital—in other words, our natural resources.

The Rocky Mountain Institute also hosts conferences on the future of oil/gas, trucking, and energy.

Silent Spring, by Rachel Carson (Houghton Mifflin, 1962). The original and definitive work on the perils of chemical pesticide use, this book was instrumental in the banning of DDT for agricultural use. I read it while living off the grid in Taos and found it to be riveting and disturbing, especially for its commentary on the interplay between the industries that manufacture pesticides and the government agencies that regulate them.

Stalking the Wild Asparagus, by Euell Gibbons (new edition, Hood, Alan C. & Company, 2005). In this reprint of his 1962 classic, Euell Gibbons recommends you pick your own wild food. Gibbons grew up during the Great Depression and helped feed his family by supplementing their meager diet with wild plants. This is a delightful, folksy read, especially if you have fond memories of the hippie era.

The Story of Stuff, by Annie Leonard (educational video), *www.storyofstuff.com*. This twenty-minute animated short film illustrates the lifecycle of all that stuff we buy here in America.

The Tightwad Gazette, *www.tightwad.com*. Those of you whose cheap streaks run deep will enjoy this source for pinching pennies. Saving money can be equivalent to saving the planet when you buy less stuff.

Unquenchable: America's Water Crisis and What to Do about It, by Robert Jerome Glennon (Island Press, 2010). This book makes an urgent case for conservation in the face of our country's water crisis. It shows the correlation between water shortages, climate change, and population growth, among other things. It also offers solutions ranging from the use of composting toilets to policy changes.

Your Money or Your Life, by Joe Dominguez and Vicki Robin (Penguin, 1992; new edition 2008), *www.yourmoneyoryourlife.info*. The original blueprint for using less stuff and reclaiming your life from the corporate treadmill, this book was my inspiration to declutter, destress, use less, and spend less.

About the Author

In October of 2006, Priscilla Short quit the stressful job she had held for a decade, broke up with her boyfriend, sold her conventional house, and moved full-time to a small, solar-powered, strawbale house in the vast sagebrush outside of Taos, New Mexico. She had no central heating, no source of electricity beyond what the sun provided, and no water supply other than what she caught on the roof. Living on savings, disconnected from both mainstream America and the national power grid, she adjusted her life throughout the next four seasons to accommodate the quirks of the house and drastically downshifted the amount of electricity, water, and other resources she consumed. By the end of a year, she discovered that what was good for her was also good for the planet, that consuming less and conserving more helps us all.

Short holds a Bachelor of Arts from Wellesley College in mathematics and a Master of Science from The College of William and Mary in operations research. She spent over a decade in the corporate world working as a systems engineer developing software to optimize the resource usage of government satellite systems. She lives in Colorado. This is her first book.

To Our Readers

Conari Press, an imprint of Red Wheel/Weiser, publishes books on topics ranging from spirituality, personal growth, and relationships to women's issues, parenting, and social issues. Our mission is to publish quality books that will make a difference in people's lives—how we feel about ourselves and how we relate to one another. We value integrity, compassion, and receptivity, both in the books we publish and in the way we do business.

Our readers are our most important resource, and we appreciate your input, suggestions, and ideas about what you would like to see published.

Visit our website *www.redwheelweiser.com* where you can subscribe to our newsletters and learn about our upcoming books, exclusive offers, and free downloads.

You can also contact us at *info@redwheelweiser.com*.

Conari Press
an imprint of Red Wheel/Weiser, LLC
665 Third Street, Suite 400
San Francisco, CA 94107